Entrepreneur MAGAZINE'S POCKET GUIDES

Why Rent? OWN YOUR DREAM HOME!

AF675864

Entrepreneur Press and
Jason R. Rich

Ep
Entrepreneur Press

Editorial Director: Jere L. Calmes
Cover Design: Beth Hansen-Winter
Editorial and Production Services: CWL Publishing Enterprises, Inc., Madison, WI, www.cwlpub.com

© 2006 by Entrepreneur Media Inc.
All rights reserved.
Reproduction or translation of any part of this work beyond that permitted by Section 107 or 108 of the 1976 United States Copyright Act without permission of the copyright owner is unlawful. Requests for permission or further information should be addressed to the Business Products Division, Entrepreneur Media Inc. Printed in Canada.

This publication is designed to provide accurate and authoritative information in regard to the subject matter covered. It is sold with the understanding that the publisher is not engaged in rendering legal, accounting or other professional services. If legal advice or other expert assistance is required, the services of a competent professional person should be sought.

Library of Congress Cataloging-in-Publication Data

Entrepreneur Press.
Why rent? own your dream home! / by Entrepreneur Press and Jason R. Rich.
p. cm.
ISBN 1-59918-035-9 (alk. paper)
1. House buying. 2. Home ownership. I. Rich, Jason. II. Title.
HD1379.E76 2006
643'.12--dc22

2006017828

12 11 10 09 08 07 06 10 9 8 7 6 5 4 3 2 1

Contents

Introduction vii

Chapter 1

Are You Ready to Become a Homeowner? 1

Are You Ready to Buy a Home? 2
Review Your Credit Reports and Obtain Your Credit Score 7
Benefits of Homeownership over Renting 16
Forming Your Home-Buying Team 18
Planning for Your Future 20
The Steps Leading to Homeownership 22

Chapter 2

Prequalifying for a Mortgage 27

Why Prequalify for a Mortgage? 28
Finding a Mortgage Broker or Lender 30
Choosing Your Lender or Broker 37
Prequalification vs. Preapproval 40
The Prequalification Process 42
You're Prequalified—Now What? 47

Chapter 3

Mortgage Mania **49**

Choose the Right Mortgage Product for Your Needs 50
Meet Mortgage Consultant Mark Giordani 53
Prime vs. Sub-Prime Credit History 68
15-, 20-, and 30-Year Fixed-Rate Mortgages 69
Adjustable-Rate Mortgage (ARM) 72
Balloon Mortgage 75
Biweekly Mortgage (aka Two-Step Mortgage) 76
More Mortgage Options for People with Less-Than-Perfect Credit 78
FHA Loans 83
Interest-Only Mortgage 85
VA Loans 88
Assumable Loans 89
Finding Your Dream Home 92

Chapter 4

Finding the Perfect Home **93**

Working with a Real Estate Agent 96
Creating a Home Tour Checklist 100
Questions to Ask a Real Estate Agent 102
Meet Thomas Stevens, President, National Association of Realtors 103
Alternative Methods for Finding Your Dream Home 112
Real Estate Web Sites Worth Checking Out 113
Deciding Where You'll Live 119
Other Things to Consider When Choosing Your Dream Home 121
Determining Your Personal Needs 125
You've Found Your Dream Home—Now What? 126

Chapter 5

Making an Offer on Your Dream Home **127**

Discovering the Value of the Home 128
Make a Formal Offer to the Seller 129
Start by Evaluating the Seller's Asking Price 133
Get the Home Appraised and Inspected Early On 134
Advice from a Professional Home Inspector 137
Negotiating Your Best Price 143
You've Agreed on a Price—Now What? 146

Chapter 6

The Purchase and Sale Agreement **147**

What Is a Purchase and Sale Agreement? 148
The P&S Gets Packed with Important Information 149
Protect Your Investment with Insurance 152
It's Time for Your Closing! 158

Chapter 7

The Closing: Congratulations! You're Almost a Homeowner **159**

What Is a Closing? 161
Be Prepared at the Closing 163
Fees Associated with the Closing 164
Navigating Through Piles and Piles of Paperwork 167
Closing-Related Mistakes to Avoid 170
Congratulations, You Are a Homeowner! 174

Chapter 8

Planning Your Move **175**

Contacting Your Current Landlord 177
Ten Tips for Packing up Your Stuff 178

Hiring a Mover or Renting a Moving Truck 180
Packing Supplies Checklist 188
Contacting Your Utility Companies 191
Get Ready for Moving Day 195

Appendix A
Web Site Directory 199

Appendix B
Glossary 204

Index 217

Introduction

Since you moved out of your parent's home, graduated from school, and landed a well-paying and stable job, have you been throwing away money on rent month after month—making your landlord richer, while not building up your equity or net worth? Are you at a point in your life where you're employed, financially, stable and ready to establish yourself as a homeowner?

Why Rent? Own Your Dream Home! is an easy-to-understand introduction to buying your first home. This book will walk you through the home-buying process, give you valuable information you need to know, provide countless tips for saving time and money, and instruct you on how to protect your personal and financial interests throughout the entire home-buying process.

While this book certainly won't make you a real estate expert, it will provide you with the insight and information you need to find and hire qualified professionals to help you with each step of the process and give you the core knowledge you need to make intelligent home-buying decisions.

Throughout this book, pay attention to the highlighted tips, warnings, and terms. These provide quick pieces of advice or extremely important information. Also, be sure to use the dozens of additional resources described throughout this book. These resources will help you save time and money, spare you unnecessary complications and hassles, and help you gain additional knowledge. Later in this book, you'll read detailed interviews with real estate professionals who will provide their personal advice, tips, and insight into what it takes to become a homeowner.

As you embark on the home-buying process, seriously consider working with a Realtor® or real estate agent who represents you, the buyer. (Throughout this book, you will be referred to as either the *buyer*, when the context relates to buying real estate, or the *borrower*, when the context rates to mortgages.) Find a lender or mortgage broker who will invest the time to ensure that you obtain the right type of financing (mortgage) to meet your needs. Hire a qualified home inspector who will evaluate your perspective home before you buy it in order to uncover any potential problems. Work with a real estate attorney who will look out for all of your legal interests and carefully explain every legal document before you sign it. You'll also want to work with a good appraiser and insurance agent or broker, a good mover, and other professionals. This book will advise you on finding the best person for each job, negotiating the best rates, and hiring the right people.

Who Are Today's Homeowners?

In the past, homeownership was reserved for middle- to high-income people with steady, well-paying jobs, excellent credit, money for a down payment, and the ability to qualify for a 15-, 20-, or 30-year fixed rate mortgage from their local bank or financial institution. Today, there are so many mortgage and financing options available that the old requirements simply no longer apply.

Today's homeowners are single professionals, newlyweds, families, single parents with kids, and retired people who were able to qualify for a mortgage. Unlike in the past, even people with poor credit or little or no money for a down payment can often qualify for some type of financing. In fact, thanks to no-income-verification mortgages, interest-only mortgages, adjustable-rate mortgages, fixed-rate mortgages, balloon-mortgage loans, and countless other financing options, more people than ever can qualify for some type of home financing, enabling them to stop throwing away money on monthly rent and begin to truly enjoy the financial and lifestyle perks of homeownership.

Why Rent? Own Your Dream Home! is all about helping ordinary people figure out whether or not they can qualify for some type of financing in order to purchase their very own home. This book will walk you through the entire process, from start to finish. The steps involved in the process of going from renter to homeowner include the following:

- Prequalifying for a mortgage (Chapter 2)
- Choosing the best mortgage option for you and applying for it (Chapter 3)
- Deciding where you want to live and what your needs are (Chapter 4)
- Finding the perfect home or condominium (Chapter 4)
- Making an offer on the property (Chapter 5)
- Completing a purchase and sale agreement (Chapter 6)
- Closing on your home (Chapter 7)
- Planning your move (Chapter 8)

This book will help you put together a qualified, reputable, and highly trained "home-buying team," so you can avoid many of the common pitfalls, mistakes, and even scams that first-time home buyers often run into as they navigate their way through the often confusing home-buying process.

While this book covers the basics on how to determine the best type of mortgage, how to get prequalified, and how to apply, for example, it's not meant to be a comprehensive resource that'll teach you everything you need to know about mortgages. Instead, you'll learn the core information you'll definitely need, then be provided with tips and strategies for finding a reputable and knowledgeable mortgage broker or lender who will be able to help you choose the best financing options based on your personal situation. You'll also learn how to find a qualified and knowledgeable Realtor® (real estate agent) to help you locate and ultimate purchase the perfect home. (A real estate agent is a Realtor® when he or she becomes a member of the National Association of Realtors®.)

Many people in America could qualify for a mortgage and become homeowners, but they don't realize it. This is often because they don't have excellent credit, a way to gather enough money for a 20-percent down payment on the property, or an employment situation for which they can document a steady income. Many people simply don't know enough about the home-buying process to even think that becoming a homeowner is a viable option. Well, chances are, if you have a steady job and you've managed to continuously pay your rent and support yourself and your family, there's probably a way for you to become a homeowner in the not-so-distant future.

Common Misconceptions About Homeownership

One of the biggest reasons why people don't consider homeownership is because they believe one or more of the common misconceptions about buying a home. Many people are under the misguided impression that homeownership isn't within their reach. These people continue to believe that the homeownership requirements that applied 10, 20, or 30 years ago still apply today.

These are some of the common misconceptions:

- You must have excellent credit (a credit score in the high 700s or better) to qualify for a mortgage.
- You must have a full-time, steady job and earn enough money to fall into the upper-middle- or upper-class income bracket.
- You need to have enough money in savings to pay at least 20 percent down.
- The month-to-month cost of homeownership is much higher than renting.
- Becoming a homeowner is too much of a responsibility and commitment.

If you haven't considered homeownership because you've believed one or more of these misconceptions, it's time to re-evaluate your situation and take steps to determine if you could qualify for one of the many types of mortgage products currently available that weren't available 10, 20, or 30 years ago. If you earn a steady income, have at least average credit (meaning a credit score over 620), and are able to afford your monthly rent, chances are you could qualify for some type of mortgage and become a homeowner.

TIP: Throughout this book, the phrase *mortgage products* refers to the many types of mortgages available from mortgage brokers and various types of lenders (banks, credit unions, savings and loans, mortgage companies, investors, government, etc.). For example, a 15-year fixed-rate mortgage and a 30-year adjustable-rate mortgage are mortgage products.

There are dozens of types of mortgages available from thousands of lenders. Hopefully, by reading this book you will discover that homeownership is within your reach. You may discover, however, that at this time, you don't yet qualify

☆ ☆ **WARNING** ☆ ☆

Unfortunately, not everyone will immediately qualify for some type of home financing and be able to buy a home after reading this book. If you don't immediately qualify for a mortgage, this book will teach you about what actions you can take in order to meet mortgage approval requirements in the future. This might mean paying off debt, boosting your credit score, being able to show a longer employment history, saving up more money for a down payment, or having inaccurate information removed from your credit report.

for the financing you'll need. Or, you may determine that taking on the responsibility of owning a home isn't right for you at this moment in your life. This book will help you make these determinations and plan your future accordingly.

The goal of *Why Rent? Own Your Dream Home!* is to help potential, qualified first-time home buyers stop throwing away money on monthly rent payments and start building up equity in their own property and boosting their net worth by becoming homeowners. Never before has homeownership been an option for so many people. If you discover you're one of these people, in the next few months, you too could find yourself living comfortably in a new home or condo.

—Jason R. Rich
www.JasonRich.com

CHAPTER 1

Are You Ready to Become a Homeowner?

WHAT'S IN THIS CHAPTER

- Determine if you are ready to become a homeowner
- Learn what's involved in becoming a homeowner
- The benefits of homeownership
- Why waste money on rent?
- Planning for your future

This chapter will help you learn what's involved in becoming a homeowner, review some of the new responsibilities you'll need to take on, and help you decide if buying a home is the right decision for you and your family. You'll also learn about some of the many lifestyle and financial benefits associated with homeownership.

Dream Home Tips

The term *home* refers to the single-family house, multi-family house, apartment, or condominium you purchase.

Are You Ready to Buy a Home?

The first step in determining if you're ready to become a homeowner is to carefully analyze your financial situation and figure out if this is something you could afford, based on current home-buying qualifications. Using a free online calculator on the Ginnie Mae web site (www.ginniemae.gov), you can quickly calculate how much you could afford to spend on your home (assuming you're able to qualify for some type of mortgage).

We'll get into the mortgage-qualification process shortly. Right now, let's focus on your financial situation to determine if you could afford to purchase a home.

Follow these basic steps:

1. Begin by calculating your total income. Gather information about all of your current sources of income and calculate your average monthly income. Do you expect this income to remain constant or to increase or decrease in the near future?

2. Calculate the amount of money you currently have in savings and investments. This will help you determine how much of a down payment (if any) you can afford. Depending on your situation, you may also need money to cover closing costs and other expenses related to purchasing a home.
3. Calculate your current monthly expenses. Are you able to cover all of your living expenses or are you going deeper and deeper into debt? If you're able to cover all of your living expenses and you're able to put some money away into savings, this will greatly improve your chances of qualifying to purchase a home. Keep in mind that once you purchase a home, some of your expenses will go up. For example, you'll need to pay your mortgage (instead of rent), insurance, and property taxes. Some of these added expenses, however, could be offset by the tax benefits associated with homeownership.
4. Evaluate your current debt. A potential lender will evaluate your debt in comparison with your income.
5. Determine your current *credit score* and review your credit reports compiled by Experian (www.experian.com), Equifax (www.equifax.com), and TransUnion (www.transunion.com). You should do this two to three months *before* applying for a mortgage.

Dream Home Vocabulary

Credit score—This is a number representing a person's creditworthiness, calculated by the three major credit reporting agencies, using a complex formula based on many criteria related to the person's current financial situation and credit history, and updated regularly. Your credit score or your credit rating is based on such things as your outstanding debt, bill-paying history, and the number and types of accounts you have and how long you have had them. According to TransUnion, a credit score is "a mathematical calculation that reflects a consumer's creditworthiness. The score is an assessment of how likely a consumer is to pay his or her debts."

When you begin applying for a mortgage, your credit and financial-related information will be evaluated by the lender. The following worksheets will help you better understand your current financial situation.

Financial Worksheet

Income	Dollars
Current Salary (including any tips, commissions, and bonuses)	$
Co-Borrower s Salary	$
Other Sources of Income (such as interest, alimony, child support, and investment dividends)	$
Total Average Monthly Income:	**$**

Savings	Dollars
Checking Account Balance(s)	$
Investments (stocks, mutual funds, etc.)	$
Retirement Fund Contribution(s)	$
Savings Account Balance(s)	$
Other Savings	$
Total Savings:	**$**

Monthly Expenses	Dollars
Car Expenses (monthly car payments, gas, repairs, insurance, etc.)	$
Child Support	$
Clothing	$
Entertainment	$
Food	$
Gifts	$
Insurance (health insurance, car insurance, life insurance, renter's insurance, etc.)	$
Medical Expenses	$
Rent	$
Utilities (electricity, gas, phone, cable, etc.)	$
Travel/Vacations	$
Other Expenses	$
Total Monthly Expenses:	**$**

Debt and Debt-Related Expenses

Monthly Expenses	Dollars
Alimony	$
Car Loan(s)	$
Child Support	$
Credit Cards (Minimum Payments)	$
Outstanding Medical Bills	$
School/Education Loans	$
Other Debt	$
Total Monthly Debt and Debt-Related Expenses:	$

Dream Home Tips

As a homeowner, you'll need to take on additional expenses, including your monthly mortgage payment (which replaces your rent payment), homeowner's insurance (which replaces your renter's insurance), property taxes, utility costs, mortgage insurance, and condominium/homeowners' association fees (if any).

As you begin searching for your dream home and then applying for financing, one of the things lenders will consider is your ability to afford and make timely mortgage payments. Two figures that will be considered are your *PITI* and *PITIO.* The *PITI* represents the principal, interest, property taxes, and insurance costs associated with your monthly mortgage payment. The *PITIO* represents the principal, interest, property taxes, insurance, and your other monthly expenses that are associated with your monthly mortgage payment.

Another number lenders will consider is your *debt ratio*, calculated as follows:

$$\text{PITIO Debt Ratio} = \frac{\rule{4cm}{0.4pt}}{\text{Total Monthly Income}}$$

Review Your Credit Reports and Obtain Your Credit Score

In addition to completing the Financial Worksheet above, contact the credit-reporting agencies (credit bureaus) and obtain a current copy of your credit report from each agency—including Experian, Equifax, and TransUnion.

Dream Home Vocabulary

Credit reporting agency (aka credit bureau)–One of the three national bureaus that maintain credit reports on virtually all Americans with any type of credit history–Equifax, Experian, and TransUnion. These agencies maintain vast databases that are updated regularly. Their purpose is to supply creditors with timely and reliable financial information about individual consumers. It's important to understand that a credit reporting agency does *not* decide whether an individual qualifies for credit or not. Credit reporting agencies simply collect information that is relevant to a person's credit history and habits and then provides that information (for a fee), in the form of a credit report, to creditors and lenders.

Credit report–Compiled by one of the credit reporting agencies–Equifax, Experian, or TransUnion–a credit report contains personal and financial information about you, including your name, address, phone number, Social Security number, date of birth, past addresses, current and past employers, companies that have issued you credit (including credit cards, charge cards, car loans, mortgages, student loans, home equity loans, etc.), and details about your credit history (whether or not you pay your bills on time.) Each of the major credit reporting agencies compiles a separate credit report for every individual. However, much of the information on each report should be identical or extremely similar.

The easiest way to do this (for free) is to visit the AnnualCreditReport.com web site (www.annualcreditreport.com). Obtaining a copy of your credit report from each credit bureau is free (once every 12 months), although you will need to pay to obtain your official credit score. (A credit score is a three-digit number that is calculated based on information in a credit report.) Knowing your credit score will help you determine whether you'll easily qualify for a mortgage or you'll have to shop around to find lenders willing to approve mortgages for people with average or below-average credit (at higher interest rates).

Dream Home Vocabulary

AnnualCreditReport.com—This is a centralized service operated by the three credit reporting agencies (credit bureaus) that processes all requests from consumers who wish to receive their free credit report from each agency. This can be done online, by phone, or by mail. To obtain your annual credit report, visit www.annualcreditreport.com.

Current Credit Score from Equifax: ______
Current Credit Score from Experian: ______
Current Credit Score from TransUnion: ______

Your credit score is an indicator of your creditworthiness. In other words, it's a tool that helps a creditor or lender gauge its risk level if it approves you for a loan or grants you credit (in this case, some type of mortgage.)

The information on your credit report includes details about your existing credit, your payment history, and other pertinent data a creditor or lender can use to make intelligent decisions about whether or not to grant you credit or approve a loan, such as a mortgage. In the past, for a creditor to make this decision, it would require a person with specialized training to carefully analyze all of the information on your credit report manually and then determine your creditworthiness. That was how things were done about two decades ago. Today, thanks to computers and the introduction of credit scoring, the process is far more automated and mortgage prequalification decisions can be made in seconds, not hours or days.

Using only information that's found on your credit report, a complex algorithm is used to calculate a credit score based on a variety of criteria, each of which is weighted differently. The result is a number between 300 and 850 that represents how much of a credit risk you are.

A credit score in the 300s or 400s is given to someone with a history of being an extremely high credit risk, while a person with a score in the mid-600s to low 700s is considered a good credit risk. Someone with a credit score in the mid- to high 700s or in the 800s is considered an excellent credit risk. These are the people who get the best deals in terms of low interest rates, for example, when applying for a mortgage, loan, or credit card.

It's important to remember that different lenders and creditors give different weight to these scores. When deciding on approving a loan or credit, here's how lenders and creditors generally perceive credit scores:

Excellent	Over 750
Very Good	720 to 750
Acceptable (Average)	660 to 719
Uncertain	620 to 659
High risk	Less than 619

You're entitled to a free copy of your credit report every 12 months, but the credit reporting agencies are not obligated to provide you with your credit score for free. Instead, they charge you for it. When you request a free copy of your credit report, you may receive an offer to purchase your credit score at the same time. For this, you'll be charged approximately $6 per score.

You can also contact each of the three credit-reporting agencies separately to purchase your credit score in conjunction with a credit report or separately. For example, from Experian, you can purchase a single credit report with corresponding credit score for $15.00 or obtain just your credit score for $5.95.

Your credit score is sometimes called your FICO® Score. FICO® is a registered trademark of Fair Isaac Corporation (NYSE:FIC), the pioneer of the FICO® credit score that's used by many lenders to evaluate consumer credit risk. According to the company's web site, "Credit reporting agency risk scores produced from models developed by Fair Isaac Corporation are commonly known as FICO® Scores. Fair Isaac credit reporting agency scores are used by lenders and others to assess the credit risk of prospective borrowers or existing customers, in order to help make credit and marketing decisions. These scores are derived solely from the information available on credit reporting agency reports. For a fee, you can obtain your FICO® Score online at www.MyFICO.com.

It's definitely a good idea to purchase your credit score at the same time you obtain a copy of your credit report. Simply by reviewing your credit report, it would be virtually impossible for you to calculate or even estimate your credit score, yet this is a vital piece of information that will ultimately determine whether or not you're creditworthy.

Each of the credit-reporting agencies (Experian, Equifax, and TransUnion) maintains a separate credit report on every consumer. The information on each credit report is often slightly different, because not all creditors and lenders report data to all three credit bureaus. Thus, when you review your three credit reports side by side, you'll notice small discrepancies, which is totally normal. Because your credit score is calculated by the data on each credit report, each of your credit scores will also be slightly different.

If your three credit scores are different, a lender will use the middle score to initially determine your eligibility for a mortgage and your interest rate. If you have only two scores available, the lower score will be used. (If you are applying with a spouse or co-borrower, the lender will use the lower of either one of your middle scores.)

When obtaining your credit score, make sure the number that you buy and receive is your official FICO® Credit Score. More than 70 percent of all lenders use an official FICO® Credit Score to make their lending and credit-approval decisions.

When you apply for a major credit card or a store credit card, for example, that creditor will check your credit history by reviewing your credit report from one of the credit-reporting agencies. Which agency they use (Experian, Equifax, or TransUnion) is their decision. In many cases, when you get a credit decision in under five minutes, that decision is based exclusively on your credit score that went along with the credit report accessed. The quick approval or rejection was an entirely automated process.

When you apply for a more substantial loan, such as a mortgage, the mortgage broker or finance company (lender) will typically access all three of your credit reports, then use the middle credit score to help make an approval decision.

Because the information on your credit report constantly

changes, as creditors report new or updated data and old data (over seven years old) drops off your credit report, your credit score from each credit-reporting agency also changes. If you're late making credit card or loan payments, for example, your credit score could drop significantly. After your score takes a dip, it's much harder and often takes longer for it to rise again.

Dream Home Tips

It's an excellent strategy to review your credit reports 60 to 90 days before applying for a mortgage. This gives you ample time to have any errors on your report corrected and to take steps to clean up your credit report before it's reviewed by potential lenders. Any erroneous or outdated information on your credit report could be dragging your credit score down. When applying for a mortgage, you want your credit score to be as high as possible so you qualify for the best deals and interest rates.

Dirty Little Secrets: What the Credit Bureaus Won't Tell You: *How to Clean Up Your Credit Report and Boost Your FICO Score* (Jason R. Rich, Entrepreneur Press, 2006) is an excellent resource for learning how to obtain, review, and—if necessary—fix your credit report and improve your credit score before you apply for a mortgage.

After reviewing your financial situation, completing the Financial Worksheet earlier in this chapter, reviewing your credit reports, and obtaining your credit score, meet with several mortgage brokers, banks, lenders, credit unions, and/or financial institutions to discuss your home financing options.

Because there are so many mortgage options and companies that specialize in different types of mortgage products, you'll definitely want to shop around and initially talk with several mortgage specialists—first to determine your options and then to find the very best deals available, based on your credit score and current financial situation.

Every time a potential creditor or lender makes an inquiry about your credit to one or more of the credit bureaus, your credit score takes a hit. However, you can work with as many mortgage brokers or lenders as you wish within a 30- to 45-day period, in shopping around for the best deal mortgage possible, and all of those credit inquiries will be combined to count as only one inquiry. This "combination deal," however, applies only to mortgage brokers/lenders and when you're shopping for a car.

As you'll learn from Chapters 2 and 3, these are some of the financial considerations in purchasing a home:

- Ensuring that your credit is good enough for you to qualify for a mortgage. Your credit doesn't have to be excellent, but it needs to be at least average—at least 620—for you to qualify. (A score in the 700s is ideal for obtaining a prime rate loan, which will be discussed later.)
- Being able to show steady employment and a regular income. There are ways of obtaining a mortgage without being able to document income. However, you will most likely need to provide federal tax returns, W-2 forms, bank statements, and pay stubs to a potential

lender during the mortgage application process.

- Accruing enough savings to afford a down payment and cover the costs associated with buying a home. These costs will vary, based on your financial qualifications and the type of mortgage. As a general rule, a down payment of 20 percent or more of the home's purchase price is standard for a conventional loan. However, there are many mortgage options that allow a significantly lower down payment or no down payment at all. There are also ways to obtain a down payment besides tapping your savings. The Federal Housing Administration (FHA) and the Department of Veterans Affairs (VA), for example, have special programs to help qualified first-time home buyers acquire the necessary down payment to purchase a home. If you qualify for a FHA loan (for your mortgage), only a three-percent down payment may be required.
- Ensuring that you'll be able to cover the ongoing costs of home ownership—mortgage payment, insurance, real estate taxes, utility bills, home maintenance and repairs, etc.
- Depending on the type of mortgage, maybe documenting that the monthly mortgage payment would represent no more than 28 to 41 percent of your monthly income. A potential lender will carefully analyze your ability to repay the loan, based on your income and

debt ratio calculations.

Dream Home Tips

The bigger your down payment, the lower your monthly mortgage payments. Your private mortgage insurance rates will also be lower and you could qualify for a lower interest rate on the mortgage by making a larger down payment or prepaying points toward the mortgage. (That's a topic covered later in this book.)

Benefits of Homeownership over Renting

Throughout this book, you will discover many benefits of owning a home as opposed to renting. These benefits include the following:

- As you pay off your mortgage from month to month, you'll be building up equity and increasing your net worth.
- You'll receive significant tax breaks as a homeowner. For example, the interest you pay on your mortgage each year is tax-deductible.
- You'll have control over your home and property and be free to make modifications and improvements without a landlord's approval.
- You'll be able to control your housing costs. With a fixed-rate mortgage, your monthly principal and interest payment will remain constant for the life of the loan. If you're paying rent, however, you can pretty much count on a rent increase from your landlord from time to time.

- You can live out the "American dream" and own property, which will hopefully go up in value over time.

As you'll soon discover, the amount of money you're currently paying for rent each month could be about the same as what your monthly mortgage payment would be if you were to purchase a home. The following chart, from the Ginnie Mae web site (www.ginniemae.gov), compares possible costs associated with buying a home and costs of renting an apartment or house. You'll see from this chart that after just a few years

Years	**Rent Payment** (includes an annual 5% increase)	**Monthly Mortgage Payment on a Home** (assumes a $110,000 purchase price)	**Monthly Difference Between Rent and Mortgage Payment**	**After Tax Savings**	**Yearly Difference**	**After Annual Tax Savings**
1	$800	$1,000	–$200	–$50	–$2,400	–$600
2	$840	$1,000	–$160	–$10	–$1,920	–$120
3	$882	$1,000	–$118	$32	–$1,416	$384
4	$926	$1,000	–$74	$76	–$888	$912
5	$972	$1,000	–$28	$122	–$336	$1,464
6	$1,021	$1,000	$21	$171	$252	$2,052
7	$1,072	$1,000	$72	$222	$864	$2,664

your monthly mortgage expenses could become significantly lower than your current rent.

Note: For information about how to best use this chart, visit www.ginniemae.gov/rent_vs_buy/Rent_vs_buy.asp?subTitle=YPTH.

According to this chart, after just three years, when you calculate the tax advantages of homeownership, the homeowner's monthly payment will be lower than the renter's monthly payment. These savings will continue to increase every year for the life of the mortgage. Remember: instead of throwing away after-tax money on paying rent to a landlord, by buying a home and making mortgage payments, you'll be building up equity in your home (a valuable asset) and continuing to boost your net worth. Plus, you'll benefit from the tax advantages associated with homeownership.

Of course, there's a lot to consider from a financial standpoint before taking on the responsibilities of homeownership. Many of these considerations will be addressed later in this book. In the next chapter, you'll learn more about mortgages, how to find the best deals, and how to apply for the type of mortgage that best satisfies your needs.

Forming Your Home-Buying Team

As you start the home-buying process, you'll need to tap the services of several professionals. Choosing the right people means obtaining the best guidance and information, which will save you time and money. The following list of experts is in alphabetical order, not in the order in which you'll need to hire them.

- Home appraiser—This professional helps to determine the current value of a home, based on a variety of criteria. The value of the home can be significantly different from the seller's asking price or the price that the buyer will ultimately pay.
- Home inspector—This professional carefully inspects the home prior to the purchase and provides a report on the condition of the home and any significant repair work that needs to be done.
- Insurance agent/broker—This specialist will help you define your home insurance needs and then sell you the appropriate policies to provide adequate coverage.
- Lender—This mortgage or finance company will provide you with the necessary funds (in the form of a mortgage) to purchase the home.
- Mortgage broker— This person acts as intermediary between you and the lender (such as a bank or financial institution), unless you deal with the lender directly. Mortgage brokers work with various lenders, so they can offer you the broadest range of mortgage products and help you choose the best one for your situation. Many mortgage brokers specialize in helping people with less-than-excellent credit get approved for some type of mortgage.
- Real estate agent or Realtor®—This professional will represent you, helping you find a home and then negotiate to purchase it. A real estate agent must be licensed

and certified. A Realtor® has the same type of license, but is also a member in good standing of the National Association of Realtors®. He or she must adhere to an additional, strict code of ethics and conduct when doing business. You'll learn more about Realtors® in Chapter 4. The seller will also be represented by a real estate agent or Realtor®, who earns a commission based on the price paid for the home.

- Real estate attorney—This attorney specializes in real estate. Both you and the seller can benefit from hiring a real estate attorney due to the significant number of legal documents and legal proceedings involved with the purchase of a home.
- Seller—This is the person selling the home, its current owner. The seller may not belong on this list of experts, because he or she is not likely a real estate professional, but certainly is an expert on his or her home.

Dream Home Tips

Depending on your situation, you may not need to work with each of the professionals on this list. For example, it's possible to find and negotiate to purchase a home without the help of a real estate agent and you could also potentially forgo a home inspection, but this is not advisable, as you'll learn in Chapter 5.

Planning for Your Future

As you're considering whether or not to pursue homeownership, one thing to consider is the real estate market where you want to live. If your job requires you to live in a certain geographic area, make sure that you can qualify for a mortgage and afford a home or condominium in or near that area. Real estate prices may be significantly lower elsewhere in the country, but that doesn't help you if you must live in or near a major city, for example, where real estate prices are exceptionally high.

To evaluate the cost of living and learn about home prices in various places throughout the United States, you can visit these web sites:

- Bankrate.com—www.bankrate.com/brm/movecalc.asp
- CityRating.com—www.cityrating.com/costofliving.asp
- CNN.com—cgi.money.cnn.com/tools/costofliving/costofliving.html
- Sperling's Best Places—www.bestplaces.net/col
- Yahoo! Real Estate—realestate.yahoo.com/re/neighborhood/mail.html

Dream Home Tips

Want to live in a more affordable area? To calculate what your salary could be in another geographic area, based on your current job title and experience, visit the Monster Board web site (promotions.monster.com/ salary) and use the free Salary Wizard.

Think of buying a home as a long-term investment in your quality of life and your future. As you do this, think about what your needs will be five, ten, and even 15 years down the road. Do you plan on getting married, starting a family, having kids? Will you need space for a home office? How much space do you need now? How much space will you need in the future? Chapter 4 will help you find a home that will best fit your needs, now and for the future.

If you're planning to relocate or you're not sure what your financial or employment situation will be like in the near future, purchasing a home right now might not be the best strategy for your financial well-being. In addition to using the information in this book, depending on your situation, consider sitting down with a personal financial planner or accountant to help you determine if buying a home in the near future is possible and whether making this type of investment would be beneficial to you.

The Steps Leading to Homeownership

You're about to begin one of the biggest and most expensive projects of your life—finding the perfect home. So much goes into finding the perfect home and purchasing it. For every first-time home buyer, the experience is unique. Your financial situation, personal preferences, needs, and the people you hire to help you through this process (such as your lender/mortgage broker, real estate agent, home inspector, and real estate attorney) will all contribute to your unique home-buying experience.

The following are some of the major steps in buying a

home. The order in which you complete these steps, like the real estate professionals you use, will vary. It's important, however, to invest the time necessary to gather all of the right information, analyze your wants and needs carefully, and then ensure that all of your legal and financial interests are protected throughout the entire process. The chapters of this book will help guide you through the steps in the home-buying process:

- Decide where you want to live. Choose a general area, based on your needs, desires, and research into cities, towns, or communities. Start with a wide area and then narrow down your search based on affordability and how much you like a specific community, for example.
- Find a reputable and experienced real estate agent. This person will educate you about the area, show you property listings, help you analyze your needs, review your financial situation, and help you negotiate with the seller.
- Determine your wants and needs in a home. How many bedrooms and bathrooms do you need, for example? Are you looking for a single-family home, a multi-family home, a condominium, or an apartment?
- Review your personal financial information to determine exactly what monthly mortgage payment and down payment you can afford.
- Find a lender, bank, credit union, financial institution, or mortgage broker. Then review your financing options with the representative and get prequalified or

preapproved for a mortgage. During this process, learn about the many types of mortgage products and financing options available to you based on your income and credit score.

- Work with a real estate agent, attend open houses, review the real estate section of newspapers, perform searches online, and talk with friends, neighbors, and coworkers to start looking at homes on the market that could meet your needs.
- Formally apply for a mortgage and line up the financing for your home. You'll want to lock in your mortgage rate and terms and then obtain a formal commitment letter from your lender.
- Prepare and submit a written offer to the seller. Your real estate agent or real estate attorney can help you prepare the formal offer.
- Negotiate with the seller to establish the final price and terms of the sale.
- Hire a home inspector to evaluate the home and its current condition. You may also need to hire an appraiser to evaluate the property's current value, based in part on current market conditions.
- Have a purchase and sale agreement (P&S) drawn up and sign it with the seller. Your real estate agent, or real estate attorney will help you create an appropriate P&S to meet your needs.
- Start planning your move by packing up your stuff,

contacting your landlord, hiring a mover, etc.

- Obtain homeowner's insurance and the other types of insurance that are required of homeowners. Some types of insurance are optional. Find a reliable insurance agent or broker to help you determine your needs and provide you with appropriate coverage.
- Prepare for the closing—the final step in the home-buying process. This is when all of the documents for the financing and sale get signed and ownership of the home passes from the seller to you.
- Move into your new home! Get acclimated with your new neighborhood and start your new life as a homeowner.

Each of these major steps in the home-buying process requires the completion of many smaller steps. Some of these will be handled by your real estate agent or other professionals you hire. It will, however, always be your responsibility to provide the people who help and/or represent you with the most timely and accurate information about your finances, personal situation, needs, and desires.

Now that you've obtained a general overview of the steps in the home-buying process, it's time to get started. Keep in mind that this process shouldn't be quick. Each step in this process takes time. For example, plan on spending at least 30 to 60 days searching for your dream home and finding a property that meets your needs and that you can afford. Investing the necessary time, doing research, and asking appropriate questions will help to ensure that you make educated decisions and then wind up happy and comfortable in your new home.

The next chapter focuses on getting prequalified or preapproved for a mortgage and better evaluating your personal financial situation, credit history, and credit score. As you'll discover, your credit history and current credit score play a tremendous role in the type of mortgage product you qualify for. This, in turn, relates directly to the fees and interest rate you'll pay for that mortgage.

CHAPTER 2

Prequalifying for a Mortgage

WHAT'S IN THIS CHAPTER

- Why prequalify?
- Finding a mortgage broker or lender
- Prequalification vs. preapproval
- The prequalification process

There are many reasons to prequalify and obtain preapproval for a mortgage prior to finding a home and then making an offer. The most important reason is that this process will help you determine exactly how much you can afford. This will enable you to narrow your home search based on financial scenarios that make sense for you.

When you begin searching for a home and potentially working with a real estate agent, some of the first questions you'll need to answer are "Where would you like to live?" and "What type of home are you looking to purchase, in terms of size and features?" and "How much can you afford?" By prequalifying for a mortgage, you'll have a price range in mind that you know you can afford, before you start searching for the ideal home.

Why Prequalify for a Mortgage?

Several important factors go into determining how much you can afford for a home, including the size of the mortgage you're qualified to obtain based on your credit history and credit score, income, savings, current debt, and employment. By prequalifying for a mortgage, you begin searching for a home knowing how much you can afford, based on the size of the mortgage you qualify for. Knowing this also allows you to easily calculate the down payment you'll need to make in order to afford the home you ultimately choose, based on the type of mortgage you'll be applying for.

Prequalifying for a mortgage will help determine where you can live and the size of your home, for example, plus save you the time of looking at properties you simply can't afford. You might want to move into a $375,000 home with a large front lawn and state-of-the-art appliances. However, you might qualify for only a $200,000 mortgage. If you can pay only $25,000 down, the maximum price of the home you should be searching for is $225,000, not $375,000. Knowing what you can afford will help you set parameters for your search.

Prequalifying for a mortgage also gives you greater negotiation leverage with sellers, especially if you're bidding against buyers who are not prequalified. If you prequalify, sellers know you potentially have the necessary funds available to purchase the homes you're considering. The chances of your financing falling through are greatly reduced. This is important if the seller is looking to sell his or her home quickly and can't afford to waste time with people who are interested but don't have the finances available to purchase the home.

Dream Home Tips

> **The amount of the mortgage** for which you prequalify plus any money from savings, for example, you plan to use as a down payment establish the maximum you can spend on the home. It is not, however, the price you should agree to pay. Always negotiate with the seller for the lowest price possible. You don't need to spend the entire amount for which you're prequalified.

Prequalifying for a mortgage is an excellent strategy for first-time home buyers. Even after you prequalify, you can still shop around for the best financing deals and continue to

> ☆ ☆ **WARNING** ☆ ☆
>
> Whatever the amount of the loan for which prequalify, it's important to develop a realistic budget and determine, in advance, that you can afford to take on that mortgage and the expenses associated with it. Remember: becoming a homeowner requires more than just making your monthly mortgage payments on time. There are also taxes, insurance premiums, possibly condo/homeowner association fees, and home repair/maintenance expenses to consider. Make sure you'll be able to afford these ongoing expenses and have funds available for furniture, landscaping, new appliances, or any other home improvements you might want to make.

explore your mortgage options. Plus, before you begin searching for a home, you'll be able to determine if you need to take steps to improve the information on your credit report, such as correct inaccuracies or pay off credit card bills, in order to boost your credit score and qualify for better mortgage rates.

As you'll discover from this chapter, prequalifying for a mortgage is easy, whether you do it with a mortgage broker or lender on the telephone, in person, or even via the Internet.

Finding a Mortgage Broker or Lender

In three words, the trick to obtaining the best mortgage is to *shop, compare,* and *negotiate* with the lender or broker. That lender could be a local bank, a credit union, a mortgage company, or some other type of financial institution. As you'll discover, organizations (such as mortgage brokers) specialize in different types of mortgage products that are suitable for different types of borrowers. Virtually all lenders are happy to work with people with excellent credit and a steady, well-paying job. If, however, you don't fall into this category (and plenty of people don't), you may need to spend some extra time shopping around for the best lender or mortgage broker to work with, in order to obtain an approval and receive the best possible rates and overall deal.

Dream Home Vocabulary

***Mortgage broker*—**This is an intermediary between the borrower and the lender. Most mortgage brokers represent multiple lenders and will work to find a lender that's most apt to approve your application, based on your unique financial and credit situation. Mortgage brokers can typically offer a broader range of mortgage products than a traditional bank. It's important to understand, however, that a mortgage broker, although working to land your business, is not obligated to give you the best rates. It's your responsibility to shop around, determine what you should be able to qualify for, and then negotiate with the broker. Mortgage brokers earn a fee for their services. These fees may be separate from the fees the lender charges. When shopping around, ask how each mortgage broker gets compensated and consider those fees. Negotiate with the mortgage broker to obtain the lowest possible fees and interest rate.

Dream Home Tips

Over 80 percent of the home buyers in the U.S. work through a mortgage broker. As of 2005, there were over 20,000 mortgage brokerage companies in America.

Dream Home Vocabulary

***Loan officer* (aka *broker associate* or *mortgage consultant*)**—The person who works for the mortgage broker who is your primary contact person through application, approval, and closing can have any of several job titles. The job description, however, is basically the same—to work with you, the borrower, and help you choose a mortgage product, help you apply for the mortgage and get approved by the lender, and prepare you for the closing. The loan officer will often work on a commission, based on the mortgage product he or she sells.

Banks, credit unions, savings and loans, and other types of financial institutions offer only their own mortgage products. As a result, their offerings and ability to negotiate rates may be limited. Because a mortgage broker represents multiple lenders, there's a lot more flexibility in terms of what the broker offers

> ☆ ☆ **WARNING** ☆ ☆
>
> Your mortgage broker should never encourage you to provide false information or inaccurate financial documents to the lender nor encourage you to leave signature lines blank on any application or loan forms. The mortgage broker should be open and honest when explaining all of the fees associated with the loan, including what he or she charges for services.

and charges. A typical mortgage broker will handle these tasks:

- Assess the borrower's circumstances, credit history, and employment situation (as appropriate).
- Help the borrower find the best mortgage product to fit his or her needs, based on current rates and offerings by lenders. This includes educating the borrower about the financing options available to him or her.
- Help the borrower get preapproved for a mortgage with one of the lenders.
- Gather all documentation (bank statements, pay stubs, tax returns, etc.) on behalf of the lender.
- Work with the borrower to complete the application form(s) for the mortgage.
- Submit the application and materials to the lender.
- Work as the liaison between borrower and lender throughout the application process and the closing.

When you start shopping around for a mortgage, you'll quickly discover that lenders and mortgage brokers will quote you different prices and rates for what appears to be the same type of loan. When comparing offers from lenders or brokers, make sure you know the loan amount, term, and type, so you can easily compare the quoted fees and rates. You'll also need to know whether the rate is fixed or adjustable. If you take an adjustable-rate mortgage and interest rates go up, so will your monthly payment. On the other hand, depending on the terms of your loan, if interest rates fall, your monthly payment might not drop.

Be sure to determine the loan's *annual percentage rate (APR).* The APR takes into account the interest rate and points, broker's fees, and other fees associated with the loan. *Points* are fees you may pay to the lender or broker; a point is one percent of the loan amount. Typically, the more points you pay, the lower your interest rate on the mortgage will be. When a lender or a broker is describing a mortgage product, ask for the points to be expressed in dollars, so you can easily determine what you're responsible to pay.

Dream Home Vocabulary

Annual percentage rate (APR)—This is the yearly rate of interest that includes all fees and costs paid to acquire the loan (such as interest, mortgage insurance, certain closing costs, and points paid at closing). All lenders are obligated by law to disclose a loan's APR.

Point—This is a fee the borrower pays to the lender or broker. It's one percent of the loan amount.

Fees are another component of a mortgage you need to be concerned about. As you'll discover, when you take on a mortgage, a wide range of fees are involved. When you begin working with a broker or a lender, ask for a summary of all fees you'll be responsible for paying. Otherwise, at the closing, you could be surprised at how much you're paying and realize you could have negotiated those fees down if you had learned about them sooner. Some of the fees you'll have to pay when you apply for the mortgage. Other fees will be due at closing or built into the loan.

Another question to ask the lender or broker early on is about the size of the down payment required to get the mortgage application approved. Depending on the type of mortgage, the down payment required could be anywhere from zero to 20 percent of the purchase price. Of course, the more money you offer as a down payment, the lower the amount of your mortgage and, thus, the lower your monthly payment.

Dream Home Tips

Interest rates for mortgages change daily. The deal you discuss on a Monday, for example, most likely will not still be available on the following Thursday or Friday, unless you take steps to lock in the rate with the lender or broker. Likewise, the same loan could be offered at different rates to different people, based on their credit histories and credit scores.

Dream Home Vocabulary

***Overage* –** The different between the lowest available rate for a mortgage and the rate you're actually quoted and agree to pay is called the *overage*. When an overage occurs, the broker or lender will keep this amount as "bonus" compensation, so it's not in his or her best interest to bring it to your attention. An overage can be a result of how the points, fees, and/or interest rate are quoted and calculated.

Dream Home Tips

Review the fees charged by the lender or broker early on and negotiate to have as many of them waived or reduced as possible in order to save money. Not all fees can be waived or reduced, but many of them can. It's these fees that often determine the profit for the lender or broker. Once you negotiate all of the fees, make sure that no fees are added and that your interest rate and/or the points you're required to pay don't increase. After you've reached an agreement with the lender or broker, you should obtain a written lock-in to ensure that what you've agreed to will be binding. The lock-in should specify the rate, summarize the fees, and state the period the lock-in will last. At this point, you may be charged a fee to lock in your rate. If rates rise before your closing, you will be protected. However, unless you negotiate this in advance, if rates fall, you could wind up paying a higher rate. Before locking in a rate, inquire about your broker/lender's *float down policy.* What this means is that, as a courtesy to you, good lenders will automatically reduce your locked-in rate, without a fee, if rates go down by a quarter percent or more within your lock-in period.

If your credit is average or below average, you may be forced to work with a high-cost lender who will charge you extra fees and offer you a higher interest rate, because you represent a greater risk based upon your credit history. If you have unusual circumstances relating to your personal finances and credit history, it's important that your lender or mortgage broker understand your situation before recommending specific mortgage products to you.

One way to potentially improve your chances of getting the best rates is to review your credit report early on and take steps to correct any inaccuracies or outdated information that could be negatively impacting your credit score. If your credit report has information that is hurting your credit score, consider paying off your creditors and/or negotiating with them to have the negative information modified or removed.

☆ ☆ **WARNING** ☆ ☆

According to Wikipedia (en.wikipedia.org/wiki/Mortgage_broker), "Another unethical practice involves inserting hidden clauses in contracts in which a borrower will unknowingly promise to pay the broker or lender to find him or her a mortgage whether or not the mortgage is closed. Though regarded as unethical by the National Association of Mortgage Brokers, this practice is perfectly legal. Often a dishonest lender will convince the consumer that he or she is signing an application and nothing else. Often the consumer will not hear again from the lender until after the time expires and then they are forced to pay all costs. Potential borrowers may even be sued without having legal defense."

In the next chapter, you will learn about some of the many types of mortgage products available, such as fixed-rated loans, adjustable-rate loans, nontraditional loans, interest-only loans, and jumbo loans. If you understand the differences among these products, you can choose which one best meets your individual needs. Once you determine this, you can shop around several lenders or brokers to find the best possible rates.

Choosing Your Lender or Broker

Finding a mortgage broker or lender is easy. They advertise everywhere! The trick, however, is finding someone who is reputable, extremely knowledgeable, and willing to work with you and invest the necessary time to help you get the best deal possible based on your personal situation. It's always a good idea to get a referral from a friend, neighbor, co-worker, or relative. Otherwise, you can find lenders and mortgage brokers online; advertising in newspapers, on radio, or on television; in the Yellow Pages; or through a referral from your real estate agent.

Dream Home Tips

Seriously consider participating in a free workshop offered by the U.S. Department of Housing and Urban Development (HUD). These workshops are offered throughout the United States on an ongoing basis. To learn more, call (800) 569-4287 or visit www.hud.gov/buying/localbuying.cfm.

The Mortgage Bankers Association (www.mortgagebankers.org) is a professional trade association of lenders and mortgage brokers. The organization publishes guidelines and requirements for its members. The "MBA Best Practices" guidelines can be found on the organization's web site. If your mortgage broker is a member of this organization, it's a good idea to review these best practices to ensure that he or she is adhering to them. They relate to compliance with state and federal laws, training, equitable treatment of clients, pricing, advertising and marketing guidelines, and other factors that can impact a borrower.

Before committing to work with a lender or a broker, check the person out with your local Chamber of Commerce and/or the Better Business Bureau (www.bbb.org). A lender or broker may advertise the best rates or make appealing statements in his or her ads, but those statements might not be true or what's offered might not be best suited to meet your needs. You'll often find that the brokers and lenders that advertise the most and have the catchiest radio and TV jingles also charge the highest fees, and they don't necessarily offer the personalized service you'll want and need as a first-time home buyer.

There are many free online mortgage comparison shopping sites. When you use one of these services, you'll be required to enter all of your pertinent personal and financial information. Those details will then be forwarded to a handful of potential brokers or lenders who will prequalify you and compete for your business. If you choose to use one of these services, you can expect to be bombarded by telemarketing phone calls, e-mails, and direct mail from potential lenders and brokers soliciting your business. While this can make shopping for the best deal easier, it can also get frustrating and annoying, since some brokers and lenders will be relentless in trying to do business with you.

Here are several popular online mortgage comparison shopping sites:

- Bankrate.com—www.bankrate.com
- HomeGain.com—www.homegain.com
- LendingTree.com—www.lendingtree.com
- LowerMyBills.com—www.lowermybills.com

As you choose your lender or broker, these should be your four primary concerns:

1. The broker can get your loan processed on time and has a good working relationship with lenders. You don't want your deal to fall through because the broker misrepresented his or her ability to get the loan approved and closed within a specified time.
2. The lender or broker has competitive rates.
3. The lender or broker is willing to offer you the best possible deal you qualify for, regardless of how much he or she earns in commissions and fees from the transaction.
4. The lender or broker you choose is knowledgeable and trustworthy.

Read Chapter 3 for additional tips for finding a reputable and knowledgeable mortgage broker or lender and strategies for working with that company or individual to obtain the best possible home financing deal.

Dream Home Tips

Ask your bank, mortgage company or broker about your *mortgage par rate*. This is the best mortgage rate you qualify to receive, based on your credit score and credit history (information on your credit reports). Ask if they are getting a *yield spread premium* for increasing your interest rate over par. If the answer is yes, this will help you determine how the lender and/or broker is earning and help you determine if you can shop around for a better rate.

Prequalification vs. Preapproval

When initially approaching a potential lender, it's important to understand the difference between being *prequalified* for a mortgage and being *preapproved*.

Prequalification is a fast, informal process. You provide the potential lender with basic financial information (without documenting it) and, based on that information, the lender will tell you approximately how much money you'd be eligible to borrow if you were to formally apply for a mortgage. You can use the prequalification process to determine what price range you can potentially afford for a home. The prequalification process can be done over the phone, in person, or online. It takes just a few minutes. However, it's not binding.

Preapproval requires the potential lender to gather financial information from you, evaluate your credit report and credit score, and review financial documents (such as tax returns, pay stubs, bank statements, and W-2 forms). If you meet the qualification requirements for the mortgage you're interested in, the lender will offer you a commitment to grant you the loan, providing that you continue to meet the same qualification requirements when you complete the full application. Some lenders will put an expiration date on a preapproval. The preapproval process takes a bit longer and will require you to complete some forms and provide financial documentation, such as tax returns, bank statements, and pay stubs.

If you take on additional debt, such as a car loan, or you lose your job after the preapproval but before the lender processes and approves your full mortgage application, there's a good chance your application will *not* be approved.

When you begin working with a potential lender, make sure that you understand what you're being offered in terms of a prequalification or a preapproval, how long it will remain in effect, and what limitations there are. Remember: everything you agree to should be put in writing.

The Prequalification Process

The prequalification process for a mortgage begins with questions that will be basically the same with any type of lender or broker. Based on the information you provide and your creditworthiness, the lender will be able to offer you mortgage options and help you choose one that you can afford and that will meet your needs.

Remember: in prequalifying for a mortgage, you are not completing the full mortgage application. This process simply gives you an idea of how much financing and the type(s) of mortgage product(s) you could obtain.

Dream Home Vocabulary

Not all lenders offer the same mortgage products. Especially if your credit history is less than excellent, you'll definitely want to shop around, not just for the best rates, but for the type of mortgage that best meets your needs.

These are some of the prequalification questions a lender will ask you:

- What is your full name? What is your current address? What are your phone numbers?
- Will you have a co-borrower? If so, you'll need to pro-

vide the co-borrower's full name, current address, and phone number(s)

- What state are you looking to buy a home in?
- What type of property are you buying (single-family home, condo, etc.)?
- How will you be using your new property (as a primary residence, vacation home, etc.)?
- Are you a first-time buyer?
- What is your gross monthly income (before income taxes) and that of your co-borrower (your spouse, if applicable)? Your income should include your base pay, bonuses, commissions, tips, overtime, child support received (if any), retirement income (if any), annuity income (if any), alimony (if any), and any other money you receive or earn on a regular basis.
- Will you be documenting your income by providing tax returns, pay stubs, etc. or will you simple state your income, but not provide documentation?
- How much cash (from all sources, including savings, investments, gifts, and assets that can be converted into cash) do you have for your down payment and closing costs? Approximately what percentage of the purchase price does this down payment represent? (For some types of mortgages, a borrower must be able to make a 20-percent down payment to qualify. For other types of mortgages, such as an FHA mortgage, the down payment can be as low as three percent of the purchase

price. Veterans who qualify for a VA loan may not need a down payment at all.)

Dream Home Tips

Your down payment must come from savings, earned income, an inheritance, or a gift. It cannot be in whole or in part through loans.

- How would you define your credit history—excellent, good, average, or poor?
- What is your approximate credit score? (If you don't know this, the lender or broker will obtain your credit report and corresponding credit score from each credit bureau.)
- What are your current debts, including auto loans, student loans, credit cards, child support, alimony payments, other mortgages, etc.?
- What is your current employment situation (including length of employment, job title, etc.)?

Based upon your income, an analysis of your debt, and your estimated down payment, your lender/broker will be

> ☆ ☆ **WARNING** ☆ ☆
>
> In most cases, a mortgage will not be approved if your credit score is lower than 620, if you have a history of being late with mortgage payments, or if you've been in your current job for less than two years. If you have a bankruptcy in your credit history, this too can keep you from being approved for a mortgage.

Based on the information you provide during the prequalification process, your *debt-to-income ratio* will be calculated. This is the amount of debt you have relative to your income. Many lenders specify a range for the debt ratio in order to qualify for their mortgage products. Fannie Mae, for example, follows the 28/38 rule, which means that to qualify for a Fannie Mae mortgage, you cannot spend more than 28 percent of your gross monthly income on housing or more than 38 percent of your gross monthly income on your monthly debt payments (that's the debt ratio), if your credit score is 620 or higher.

able to calculate the maximum mortgage amount you could qualify for. This process is often called a *prequalification analysis*. It is meant to provide you with a rough idea of how much you could borrow. Once you provide the necessary information, including answers to the previous questions, the prequalification process should take just minutes. Be as accurate as possible, so the resulting figure is a realistic indication of what you can afford.

The prequalification analysis will generally remain valid for between 30 and 90 days, depending on the lender. Until you provide detailed information to the lender and complete a full application, however, it is not guaranteed that you'll be approved for the mortgage or that you will receive the interest rate being discussed.

Chapter 3 delves deeper into the process of applying for a mortgage, which is much more time-consuming and in-depth than prequalifying. Completing a full mortgage application will take approximately an hour and require providing the lender/broker with financial documents, including tax returns, W-2s, pay stubs, and bank statements.

Dream Home Tips

There should be no cost or commitment required when you begin working with a lender on a prequalification analysis. Based on the results of this analysis, the lender should be able to offer you a variety of mortgage products that you'd qualify for. However, if you choose to initiate the mortgage-application process, there will be a fee of several hundred dollars.

If you choose to pursue preapproval (not just prequalification), you'll need to provide your Social Security number and that of any co-borrower and agree to allow the lender/broker to obtain your credit reports from the three credit bureaus.

Dream Home Tips

There are hundreds of mortgage products out there, beyond the traditional 15-, 20-, and 30-year fixed-rate mortgages offered by banks. Each type of loan and each lender have a different set of qualifications and approval guidelines. Even if you don't qualify for one type of mortgage, you may easily qualify for another. Work with one or more lenders/brokers to learn about all of the options available to you. If your credit history is below average, you may still qualify for a mortgage. However, the terms of that mortgage won't be as good as the terms offered to someone with excellent credit. Someone with below-average credit could wind up paying tens of thousands of dollars extra over the life of the mortgage.

Traditional banks are a lot tougher in their approval process than most other types of mortgage brokers and lenders. Unless you have excellent credit and an established relationship with a bank, you can often save a lot of money and be more easily approved for a mortgage if you shop around and approach mortgage brokers and lenders other than traditional lenders (such as banks).

Remember: a loan officer working for a mortgage broker is an intermediary between you and the lender(s) he or she represents. The mortgage broker is typically not the actual lender and does not make the final approval decision for the loan.

You're Prequalified—Now What?

Once you've found a mortgage broker, bank, financial institution, or lender to work with and you have a general idea of mortgage you'd qualify for, you can begin searching for the perfect home.

It's easy for first-time home buyers to get confused or overwhelmed by all of the types of mortgage products out there. You'll also need to figure out how to obtain the best financing deal possible, find the perfect home, and negotiate the best purchase price with the seller. Since you're not a real estate expert, learn as much as you can from this book, but be sure to surround yourself with a lender/broker, a real estate agent, and a real estate attorney, people whom you trust and who can offer their guidance as you work your way through this entire process. Remember: it's OK to ask lots of questions and to check and recheck all of the information that's provided to you.

Never allow yourself to be tied to a mortgage or pushed into purchasing a home that you simply can't afford, even if you find a lender willing to approve you for the mortgage needed to purchase the home. It's your responsibility to calculate your budget and perform some financial calculations yourself to ensure that you're not taking on too much debt or overextending yourself financially in the short or long term. A mortgage is typically a commitment of 15, 20, or 30 years. If you fail to meet that commitment down the road, you could end up facing foreclosure and/or in serious debt.

In the next chapter, you'll learn all about the various types of mortgage products available and read an interview with a well-respected loan officer who works for a mortgage broker. This loan officer shares his "insider" information and provides advice for first-time home buyers.

CHAPTER 3

Mortgage Mania

WHAT'S IN THIS CHAPTER

- The mortgage information you should know
- Basics of some of the many mortgage options
- Tips from a mortgage consultant

As soon as you sit down with a mortgage broker, mortgage company, bank, credit union, savings and loan, other financial institution, or other lender, one of the first things you'll discover is that you have many options in choosing the best mortgage to meet your needs.

Dream Home Tips

While you'll receive guidance from your mortgage specialist, it's always smart to shop around and speak with multiple lenders or brokers *before* choosing that specialist.

Choose the Right Mortgage Product for Your Needs

These are some of the considerations that you should take into account as you choose the type of mortgage to apply for:

- Your credit score and the information on your credit report
- Your ability to make a down payment
- The type of home you're purchasing
- Your current financial situation and ability to make the monthly mortgage payments and afford the real estate taxes, insurance, and other expenses
- Your ability to provide proof of employment, tax returns, pay stubs, bank statements, and other financial records to the lender
- The stability of your financial situation (Do you anticipate a reduction in your income or a change in your employment situation in the near future?)

- The length of time you plan to live in the home you're interested in buying

This chapter focuses on the plethora of mortgage options available to borrowers. As you read this chapter, it's important to remember that not all home buyers will qualify for each type of mortgage. Also remember:

- Some mortgage products are more suitable for people in specific financial or employment situations.
- Different mortgage brokers and lenders have different qualification requirements and approval guidelines for each of their mortgage products.
- Each broker or lender will offer you a slightly different selection of mortgage product options, with brokers offering the largest selections of products because they typically represent a variety of lenders.

For each type of mortgage product described in this book, you'll read a brief description of how the mortgage works and

> ☆ ☆ **WARNING** ☆ ☆
>
> This chapter describes some of the most common mortgage options. However, brokers and lenders may offer you additional mortgage products or variations on the common mortgage products described here. Before completing an application, make sure you understand the specific mortgage product you're applying for. Some of the things to look out for will be described within this chapter.

learn about some of the pros and cons and the type of borrower it might appeal to. Because every home buyer's situation is different, once you understand the basic information provided here, be sure to have a detailed discussion with your mortgage broker or lender about your specific options.

These mortgage products and options apply to first-time home buyers. For people who are refinancing a mortgage or who have purchased a home in the past, for example, additional mortgage products and other financing options may be available.

Dream Home Tips

Review carefully the truth-in-lending, good-faith estimate, and HUD-1 statements provided by the lender or broker before your closing. These documents will outline all of the fees you'll be paying associated with the loan. Because not all fees are listed on each document, it will be necessary to review and compare information on all three documents to get a clear picture of all fees and charges you're responsible for. Your real estate attorney is an excellent resource for guidance if you need information on any of these documents explained.

Dream Home Vocabulary

Truth-in-lending statement (TIL)—This is a document provided by a lender to a mortgage applicant that details information about the mortgage, including the estimated monthly payment and all of the costs associated with the loan, including finance charges. If any of these figures change prior to the closing, the lender will revise the TIL and provide the update to the buyer at the closing.

Good-faith estimate—This is an estimate of all closing fees, including prepaid and escrow items and lender charges, that the lender or mortgage broker must provide to the borrower within three days after he or she applies for a loan.

HUD-1 Settlement Statement—This is a document prepared by the closing agent that details all of the information relating to the sale of the home, including price, amount of financing, loan fees, loan-related charges, real estate taxes due, and amounts to be paid by the seller and the buyer. Federal law states that you can request a copy of the HUD-1 to review 24 hours prior to the closing. All of the information on the HUD-1 should correspond to the details in the *good-faith estimate* and *truth-in-lending statement.* At the closing, both the seller and the buyer sign this document; the lender keeps the original.

Principal—The amount of money you borrow, not including interest, taxes, or insurance premiums associated with the mortgage.

Meet Mortgage Consultant Mark Giordani

Mark Giordani is a senior mortgage consultant with one of the largest privately owned mortgage brokerage firms and correspondent lenders in the United States. Acting as a personal "mortgage shopper," his job is to help his clients determine their mortgage needs and apply for the most suitable mortgage and then to oversee the mortgage process—from prequalification to closing.

Because he works for a well-established and large mortgage brokerage and correspondent lender, he has access to dozens of lenders offering hundreds of mortgage products. In this interview, Giordani offers advice to first-time home buyers on the mortgage application process and working with a broker. Later in this chapter, he also offers his insight about specific types of mortgage products.

Based in Massachusetts, Giordani works with a broad range of clients from across America, including first-time home buyers. He can be reached at (888) 695-3353 or (508) 291-8000.

What is a mortgage broker?

Mark Giordani: "A mortgage broker is just like a Realtor®, except instead of helping you find the perfect home, a mortgage broker helps you find the perfect home financing option, based upon your unique situation. The mortgage broker's job is to collect specific information from you, then utilize that information to find you the best mortgage product you'd qualify for. The benefit of working with a broker is that they have relationships with many different lenders, so they typically have access to a much broader range of mortgage products. If you work with a bank or a mortgage lender directly, you're limited to only the mortgage products offered by that one company."

What's the best way to find a reputable and knowledgeable mortgage broker?

Mark Giordani: "The very best way to find a mortgage broker is through a referral from someone you know and trust, who has had a good working relationship with their broker. Positive word-of-mouth referrals are one of the main ways I acquire new clients. If you can't find a good referral from someone you know, sit down with three or four different brokers before choosing one to work with."

Is there anything that makes one mortgage brokerage different from another?

Mark Giordani: "There are many things that distinguish one mortgage brokerage firm from another. The first is size. Most often, the larger mortgage brokerage firms do more volume of business with the banks they represent. This often means that they have lower rates that can be passed on to you. In addition, larger mortgage brokerage firms tend to be licensed in more states. You have to be sure that the company you are working with meets the appropriate licensing guidelines in your state. Also, many mortgage brokerages function as 'correspondent lenders.' What this means is that the mortgage brokerage company is actually going to close your loan in the name of their company. It also means that your entire loan process from application to processing to underwriting and closing will all be done in house.

Dream Home Vocabulary

Correspondent lender—In addition to mortgage brokers and direct lenders, you'll also find hybrid companies that offer borrowers the benefits of working with a direct lender and the flexibility of working with a broker who represents many mortgage products. A correspondent lender makes approval decisions and initially funds the loan, as a mortgage banker or direct lender would. Upon closing the loan, however, the correspondent lender then sells the loan to another lender for servicing. As the borrower, you'll be dealing with the banker who will be funding your loan right from the start, yet who will be able to shop your mortgage around to find you the best rates and terms. Typically, a correspondent lender will offer more competitive rates than ordinary brokers. When shopping around for a broker or lender, ask if the company is a correspondent lender.

"Working with a broker that is established as a 'correspondent lender' can offer big advantages to you, not only in rates and terms, but also in speed and efficiency. Because the brokerage company is functioning directly as a lender, they can identify problems much earlier in the process that would otherwise not be caught until later with other firms. Look for a correspondent lender as your broker whenever possible. If timing is critical, correspondents can get things done cheaper and faster than their broker counterparts."

What type of personal or financial information should a borrower be prepared to provide during an initial conversation with a mortgage broker?

Mark Giordani: "During the initial conversation, provide as much basic information about your unique situation as possible. This doesn't mean, however, that you must provide all of the details pertaining to your personal financial information right away. At some point, you will need to provide your date of birth and Social Security number so the broker can review your credit, but this should happen after you develop a comfort level working with that broker. Initially, your broker should be provided with an overview of what you hope to do. In other words, just tell them what your plans are."

Should a first-time home buyer seek out a prequalification before starting the mortgage application process?

Mark Giordani: "I recommend getting prequalified as a first step, because this will make you a more attractive buyer to Realtors® and sellers. Once you go through the prequalification process and then start looking for a home to purchase, you should begin the preapproval or full mortgage-application process. While a mortgage company will do an analysis to determine how much house you can afford, I don't recommend trusting their numbers. In reality, what the banks and lenders do is determine the *maximum* that they are willing to lend to you. The banks do not take into consideration that you may want to be paying for other things than just your mortgage. They do not consider that you may want to be saving for school tuitions or that you want to be able to take vacations or go out to eat. You have to determine how much you want to afford for your new home.

"A good broker can help you, but ultimately, it is your money. You know best what kind of lifestyle you want to have after you purchase your new home. Don't let any lender tell you how much to spend on a new home."

What services should someone expect from his or her mortgage broker?

Mark Giordani: "One of the biggest complaints people have about some mortgage brokers is their lack of accessibility and follow-through. They're too busy to return phone calls and they're never available to answer questions. A good mortgage broker is someone you should be able to pick up the phone and call. If you need to leave a message, it should be returned in a timely fashion. If you find a mortgage broker isn't attentive to your needs, find someone else to work with right away.

"It is helpful to know that a mortgage broker's job is a very active one and a good mortgage broker can go from very available to extremely busy within just few days, based on rapidly changing market conditions and the number of closings they might have in a given week. If you generally find your mortgage broker to be responsive, do not panic if he takes a little extra time to return a particular call. Mortgage brokers juggle the needs of many clients simultaneously and develop a sense of prioritizing to handle truly urgent issues. Sometimes less time-sensitive matters need to wait.

"That being said, find someone who is willing to take the time to answer all of your questions. Many people are under the impression that when they work with a mortgage broker, they're simply buying a product—the mortgage. This isn't the case. They're also buying a service. It's the service the mortgage broker provides that'll help the borrower choose a mortgage product, complete the application-and-approval process, and oversee the entire home-financing process from start to finish. The borrower's goal should be to establish a working relationship with their broker. Find someone who is willing to invest the time needed to answer all of your questions. If someone is reluctant to educate you, address your concerns, and answer your questions, seek out a different broker immediately."

At what point should someone lock in his or her rate with the mortgage broker?

Mark Giordani: "Rates are constantly changing in the mortgage business. This is not something the mortgage broker controls. If you wait to lock in the terms of your loan, rates can stay the same, go up, or go down. Locking in your rate protects you for a predetermined period of time and ensures you'll get that rate, even if they go up. Make sure that the time period you lock in your rate for is long enough for you to complete the mortgage-application process, find a home to purchase, handle your negotiations, and complete the closing process. If the duration of the lock isn't long enough, you'll wind up potentially having to pay for costly extensions. There's no harm in locking your rate early, as long as you know you may need to obtain an extension.

"A broker will charge anywhere from nothing to $500 to lock in a rate. In some cases, this lock-in rate will also include the cost of the appraisal once you've selected a home. This fee is taken to cover the costs the mortgage broker will need to incur to pull your credit report and hire the appraiser, for example. In some cases, it is refundable. Rates locks are available for periods of up to one year, possibly longer, so you don't need to worry about getting the rate that's right for you.

"A reputable firm will actually reduce your rate during the lock period if the rate goes down between the time you locked and when your loan closes. Ask about the broker's or lender's 'float-down' policy for details. A lock protects you from the rate going up, but if the rate goes down after you lock, you can often float down and be protected from that. Just remember: you can't generally lock a rate until you have the property address of the property you plan to purchase. There are, however, one or two programs that let you lock and then find a property. A good broker can find you one."

How much discretion does a mortgage company have when it comes to determining your interest rate and fees?

Mark Giordani: "Banks and lenders look for different things in terms of the qualifications of the borrower. Lenders make their approval decisions based on three things: the borrower's credit, collateral, and character. The credit information comes directly from the credit bureaus. The collateral is determined by your down payment and the value of the property being purchased. This is why an appraisal is usually needed. The borrower's character refers to such factors as your past housing history and employment history. These three factors combined will help determine the interest rate and loan terms a lender is willing to offer the borrower.

"If someone's credit is challenged due to late payments on a car loan, student loan, or credit cards, for example, this may negatively impact the rate the borrower is going to be offered. The loan-to-value calculation will also help determine the interest rate. If the borrower is making a large down payment, this will often allow the lender to offer a better interest rate or more desirable terms. Essentially, as the risk goes up for the lender, the higher the interest you're going to pay.

Dream Home Vocabulary

Loan-to-value (LTV)—This is the ratio between the amount of the loan and the value of the property. Many types of mortgages have a specific LTV as a requirement for approval. If you're buying a home and making a 20-percent down payment, your LTV would be 80 percent. If you're making a five-percent down payment, your LTV would be 95 percent.

"Within a specific person's scenario, the broker does have some discretion on the rate and terms offered. This is, in part, based on how much profit the broker wants to earn. It's important for the borrower to understand that, while the rate and some fees are often somewhat negotiable, not all fees are negotiable. There are definite limits as to how much discretion a broker has. Many of the fees that are charged on a loan transaction are actual out-of-pocket fees that the lender has to pay in order to get the transaction completed. Since they are not marked up, there is often no room for negotiation on them.

"If the broker is charging a loan-origination fee or points, these are typically the fees that can sometimes be negotiated. Because the mortgage brokerage company I work for is so large, they have very well established relationships with attorneys, appraisers, and title companies. Because we do such a large volume of business with these service providers, our fees for these services are typically quite low. We pass on that savings to our clients."

How much of a time commitment for the borrower to apply for and get approved for a mortgage?

Mark Giordani: "One of the frightening things for first-time borrowers is that they don't know the answer to this question. The thing to understand is that this is a process and it takes time. A good mortgage broker should be able to explain to you what the process is upfront, and then be able to tell you want to expect during each step of the process based on your unique situation.

"How long the process takes will vary based on your situation and the type of mortgage product you're applying for. A lot also has to do with how quickly the borrower provides the necessary documentation needed to get their application approved. It's also important to understand that during this process, if you're asked for specific types of financial documents, this is a standard procedure. You are not being singled out. Different lenders require different documentation, based on the type of mortgage being applied for. The lender will often request additional documentation throughout the application and approval process."

To prepare for the mortgage-application process, what type of paperwork should the borrower begin to gather?

Mark Giordani: "If you'll be using your income and assets to qualify and you're looking for the lowest rate mortgage possible, one of the best things you can do is collect your pay stubs for the past 30 days, obtain copies of W-2 forms for the past two years, if you're not self-employed, otherwise two years of tax returns will be required, and gather your bank statements that reflect the balances in your checking and savings accounts for the past two months. You'll also want to provide two months' worth of statements for investment accounts and IRAs, for example. Two years of your employment and housing history is also typically a requirement.

"If you have potential challenges with your credit, income, or employment, it's very tempting to sugarcoat this information when explaining it to the broker. This is a mistake. The broker needs an accurate picture of your situation in order to get you the best possible deal. Anything you say that isn't accurate will be discovered later on when various documents are requested and reviewed. If the broker has you apply for a loan based on information you provide, but the documents don't support what you've said, your chances of having your application denied increase dramatically. Fortunately, there are, however, loan products available for almost any type of situation. It's important to obtain a loan you qualify for and one which you can ultimately afford. By providing accurate information, you'll save time, frustration, and money by allowing the broker to fit you with a loan that's best suited to your situation.

"It is also important to know that, just because you are asked to document something, it is not necessarily because there is a problem. A mortgage decision can be a complicated one for a lender to make. Often they ask for proof of something, not because they doubt your word, but because they need to have it be part of your loan file for someone else in the process to see.

"The best time to discuss potential problems with your credit, income, or employment is during the prequalification process, not once you're completing a formal application for a specific loan you might not actually qualify for.

The documentation you supply must match the information you initially provide to the broker.

"Lastly, the temptation to fudge a loan application or parts of your income or employment history can be too strong for some borrowers. Banks have underwriting guidelines that they've spent millions of dollars to create. These guidelines are actually very lenient, but are based on the data from hundreds of thousands of loans that have gone bad in the past. If by telling the truth you can't get a loan, don't take the loan. You will be protecting yourself from a possible nightmare down the road. If you can't meet one of the flexible programs that are being offered, you may want to think twice before promising to pay back a loan you may not be able to afford. Banks are eager to loan you money. They make money by charging you interest. If they don't want to lend based on your circumstance, it is because they don't think they will get their money back. What would this mean to you? Foreclosure possibly ... and maybe worse."

What are some of the pitfalls a borrower should look out for early on when dealing with a mortgage broker?

Mark Giordani: "It's common for a borrower to call around and do some rate shopping. If you keep making enough calls, it's not uncommon to find a loan officer or broker who is going to either lie to you or who is incompetent. Without actually reviewing key financial information and documents that you provide, no mortgage broker can promise you an approval for any type of mortgage. If you pick up the phone and ask for a company's best rate on a 30-year, fixed-rate mortgage, they may quote you a very low and competitive rate, but that's not necessarily the rate you'll ultimately qualify for.

"Your best bet is to find an established and reputable broker who will then gather key financial information upfront so that they can provide you with the most accurate rate quote possible based on your qualifications. Otherwise, the quote they provide ultimately means nothing.

"While the Internet can be helpful in getting a mortgage, be careful. Clients that call me directly can most often get better pricing than they may have gotten if they came through to me via some of the popular loan-shopping tools. This is because if they come directly to us, we don't have to pay fees and commissions to the lender search service they signed up for, and I can pass the savings directly to the consumer."

What's the lowest credit score someone can have in order to qualify for a loan?

Mark Giordani: "This is a tricky question. There are so many different mortgage products available, someone with a credit score in the low 500s can potentially get approved for some type of loan, but the rate will be higher than for someone with a higher credit score. Different credit scores allow borrowers to qualify for different loan programs. As the risk increases for the lender, the rates and fees get higher.

Your chances of approval and being able to get a more competitive rate increase greatly with a credit score over 620. To get the best rates and terms, a credit score in the 700s or 800s is most desirable."

What is the biggest scam to watch out for when working with a mortgage broker?

Mark Giordani: "One of the biggest things to look out for is a broker who states you qualify for a mortgage at a very desirable rate without obtaining your prequalification information and reviewing your actual financial documentation first. A broker will need details about your credit, finances, and employment before being able to provide even a ballpark figure as to what you qualify for. There is probably no lender that can accurately tell you what you will qualify for, if you're inquiring about a full documentation loan, that hasn't seen any of your documents, credit, or employment history.

"As a general rule, anytime a deal seems too good to be true, it probably is. The mortgage business is a very competitive industry. If the price of gold is currently $300 per ounce, but someone is willing to sell it to you at $200 per ounce, there is probably a reason to be suspicious. The same is true with mortgages. If a broker offers you a significantly lower rate than other brokers, beware and make sure you understand all of the terms of that loan. Protect yourself by getting everything in writing and carefully reviewing your good-faith-estimate and HUD-1 statement."

If a borrower feels uncomfortable with the mortgage broker he or she begins working with, at what point can that person walk away?

Mark Giordani: "A borrower can typically walk away at any point up until the closing. However, they run the risk of losing their deposit, appraisal fee, and/or lock fee. You may be responsible for any out-of-pocket expenses the mortgage broker has incurred. Just because you can walk away from the loan transaction, you may not, however, be able to walk away from the purchase and sale agreement you've signed with the seller. Before walking away, be sure to consult with your attorney, especially if a purchase and sale agreement has already been signed."

Prime vs. Sub-Prime Loans:

Now that you know what's involved in working with a mortgage broker or lender to apply for a loan, the remainder of this chapter focuses on specific types of mortgage products. As you read about each type of mortgage product, Mark Giordani shares some insight about the pros and cons of each.

Borrowers with excellent credit and verifiable income often qualify for the best deals in mortgages. These borrowers qualify for the best terms and interest rates. These are considered "prime" or "A paper" loans. While many people might not qualify for a prime loan (for any number of reasons), there are a variety of sub-prime loans available. Many mortgage brokers and lenders specialize in catering to the needs of sub-prime borrowers. While a sub-prime borrower will typically pay a higher interest rate and higher fees to obtain a mortgage, getting approved is still a definite possibility.

***Sub-prime borrower*—**This is someone who doesn't meet the approval guidelines for a prime rate mortgage. This could be due to a below-average credit score, a negative credit history, lack of employment information, an inability to provide financial documents or verifiable income, or even a bankruptcy.

***Sub-prime lender*—**This is a lender or mortgage broker that specializes in working with sub-prime borrowers and offers home financing options that have less strict or nontraditional approval guidelines.

15-, 20-, and 30-Year Fixed-Rate Mortgages

This is the most common and traditional type of mortgage. Not long ago, it was also the only type of mortgage product available; prospective home buyers either qualified for it or not. Today, with so many mortgage products available from a wide range of financial institutions and lenders, this is no longer the case.

A fixed-rate mortgage has an interest rate that remains the same for the term of the mortgage. The longer the term, the lower your monthly payment will be, because you have more time to pay back the principal. The longer the term, however, the more interest you'll pay over the life of the loan, even though your monthly payments are lower. The higher your credit score and the more you put down (and a few other factors), the lower the interest rate.

Take a look at the following example of 15- and 30-year fixed-rate mortgages for a $200,000 loan at 7.5 percent.

> 15-Year Fixed-Rate Mortgage
> (180 monthly payments, excludes taxes and insurance)
> Monthly Payment: $1,854.03
> Total Interest Paid over Life of Loan: $133,729.00
> 30-Year Fixed-Rate Mortgage
> (360 monthly payments, excludes taxes and insurance)
> Monthly Payment: $1,398.43
> Total Interest Paid over Life of Loan: $303,425.00

As you can see, extending the term of the loan decreases the monthly payment but increases the amount of interest. A simple amortization table or calculator will show how much of the monthly payment is being applied to the principal and how much is for interest. When reviewing a fixed-rate mortgage, print out an amortization table for the loan to see how much of your monthly payments will be applied to the loan's principal and how much to interest from month to month throughout the term of the loan.

Dream Home Vocabulary

Amortization–This is the repayment of a loan, such as a mortgage, where part of the payment is applied to the principal balance and part is interest. The more money that's applied to the principal over time, the lower the interest payment becomes and the more equity the borrower builds.

Take the above example of the fixed-rate, 30-year mortgage of $200,000 at 7.5 percent interest with monthly payments of $1,398.43 for the term of the loan. Using an amortization calculator, you can see that only $148.93 of the first payment would be paying off the principal, while $1,250.00 would be paying interest. Almost 30 years later, with the final payments, less than $20 of each payment would be interest and the rest would be paying off the principal. You can find a free amortization calculator on many real estate web sites, including realestate.yahoo.com/calculators/amortization.html.

Fixed-rate mortgages are typically available for 10-, 15-, 20-, and 30-year terms from most lenders. As always, you'll want to shop around for the best rates, terms, and options.

Words of Wisdom from Mortgage Consultant Mark Giordani

"A fixed-rate mortgage is a great product if someone will be living in or owning the property for a long time. A fixed-rate mortgage is an amortized loan. Every month when you make your mortgage payment, some portion of it will go toward the principal and some to the interest.

Historically, this has been a very popular loan choice, but has become less popular due to the variety of mortgage products now available."

Adjustable-Rate Mortgage (ARM)

An adjustable-rate mortgage (ARM) has an interest rate that can change during the life of the loan. If the interest rate goes down, so does the monthly payment (in most cases). If the interest rate goes up, so does the monthly payment. The benefit to this type of loan is that the initial rate could be significantly lower than the rate for a comparable fixed-rate mortgage. This makes becoming a homeowner more affordable (in terms of monthly payments) and often makes qualifying easier.

These loans, also called *variable-rate loans*, have been popular since the late 1980s. The big drawback to this type of loan is that the interest rate changes constantly and the borrower is basically gambling that it will go down, not up. However, depending on the lender, you may not benefit if rates go down, but you will be penalized if rates go up.

There are mortgage products that start off at a fixed rate for the first few years, then automatically switch to an adjustable rate. This type of loan, the *fixed/adjustable mortgage*, is good if you have an average or below-average credit score, because you can qualify for a loan at a lower interest rate than for a traditional fixed-rate mortgage. During the initial one, two, three, or five years, when the rate is fixed, you can work toward improving your credit score. Then, before the loan transforms into an adjustable rate-mortgage, you can refinance and potentially qualify for a fixed-rate mortgage at a more attractive rate, assuming that interest rates haven't gone up much.

Some lenders offer *hybrid* or *convertible ARMs* that start off as adjustable-rate mortgages and then can be transferred into fixed-rate mortgages after a sprcified period. Again, however, the borrower is gambling that rates will stay the same or drop, not rise, during the specified period.

Because ARMs come in a variety of configurations, make sure you fully understand the mortgage product you're being offered. If the mortgage will start off as a fixed-rate mortgage and automatically transform into an ARM, you want to know exactly what the fixed-rate period will be and then how often the rate will adjust thereafter. Will the loan include preset caps on the adjustable interest rate?

☆ ☆ WARNING ☆ ☆

Before agreeing to an adjustable-rate mortgage, consult with several lenders or mortgage brokers and determine what your monthly payments will be immediately and what they could be if rates increase. While the initial offer for this type of loan may be attractive, make sure it makes sense over the long term based on your financial situation.

Words of Wisdom from Mortgage Consultant Mark Giordani

"When a bank is committing to a fixed interest rate for 10, 15, 20, or 30 years, there's a good chance that interest rates may rise, but the bank will not be able to pass that raise along to you. If a loan carries an adjustable interest rate, lenders are usually willing to offer a lower rate than they would for a fixed-rate mortgage. Because it's an adjustable rate, the lender can later raise the interest rate after one, two, three, or five years (or sooner—be careful!), for example, based on the predetermined guidelines of that loan. An ARM can save you money if it has a fixed rate for several years and you know you don't plan to hang onto that property for that entire fixed-rate term.

"For example, if the ARM has a fixed rate for the first five years, but you only plan to keep the home for four years, you can qualify for a lower interest rate for those four years and save money. The risk to you is that if you wind up keeping the property beyond the five years, your interest rate could go up, which means your monthly payment will increase. This can work the other way too. To your advantage, adjustable-rate mortgages can also adjust in a downward fashion."

Balloon Mortgage

A balloon mortgage has one final payment that is much higher than the regular monthly payment. The borrower receives a lower rate and makes lower monthly payments for a specific period of time, which can typically be between three and ten years. After that period, the borrower must pay off the principal balance in one lump sum. At this point, under certain circumstances, the loan could be converted to a fixed-rate or adjustable-rate loan through refinancing. This type of mortgage product is best for people who plan to sell their home, pay it off, or refinance it *before* the balloon payment comes due. It's potentially a good short-term loan option for people who qualify, because monthly payments are typically significantly lower than with more traditional types of loans. Homebuyers will benefit even more if the property appreciates in value.

The drawback to this type of loan is that when the final, balloon payment is due, if you plan to refinance the loan to transform it into a fixed-rate mortgage, the interest rate could be much higher than when you obtained the loan.

Before getting any type of nontraditional loan, shop around for the best deal and consult with a financial planner and/or several lenders or mortgage brokers to ensure that you understand the specific terms you're being offered and that this type of loan is most suitable for your individual needs, based on your financial and credit circumstances. There are so many other products on the market that it is best to stay away from balloon loans, unless there is no other option and you fully undersand the extent of the risks involved.

> *Words of Wisdom from Mortgage Consultant Mark Giordani*
>
> "Balloon loans tend to have a lot of stigma attached to them. If you don't have the money for that final large payment, the lender could foreclose on the property. Generally speaking, if you can qualify for a non-balloon loan, I would pursue that option instead. Discuss your options with your mortgage broker or personal financial advisor."

Biweekly Mortgage (aka Two-Step Mortgage)

A biweekly mortgage works just like a traditional fixed-rate mortgage, except that, instead of making payments every month, the borrower makes lower payments biweekly (every two weeks). Paying biweekly means 26 payments a year—the equivalent of 13 months. The benefit is that you would pay off the loan significantly faster than a standard fixed-rate loan and pay much less interest over the life of the loan. You would also be building up equity in your home much faster and could cut the time it takes to pay it off by up to eight years.

Often, the lender deducts the biweekly payments automatically from the borrower's checking account. The main drawback to this type of loan is that you must be able to afford to make the payments every two weeks. Your ability to do this will most likely be impacted by how you're paid at your job.

Let's use the example of a 30-year, $200,000 fixed-rate mortgage with a 7.5-percent interest rate. The monthly payment would be $1,398.43 (excluding taxes and insurance). With biweekly payments, each payment would be half—$699.21 (again excluding taxes and insurance). In one year, the payments would total $16,781.16 if monthly ($1,398.43 times 12) and $18,179.46 if biweekly ($699.21 times 26)—a difference of $1,398.30. By paying biweekly rather than monthly, instead of paying approximately $303,425 in interest over the life of the loan, you'd pay only about $225,321. You'd save over $78,104. You'd also pay off the loan 6.5 years sooner—in 23.5 years instead of 30.

For those who can afford to make the biweekly payments, this can be a very attractive opportunity. Another option is to accept a standard fixed-rate loan that has no penalties for prepayment and to make one or more additional payments toward the principal each year. This strategy too will pay off the loan faster and save you a fortune in interest over the term of the mortgage.

Dream Home Tips

Some companies refer to biweekly mortgage products as "mortgage savings programs." The qualifications are basically the same for this type of loan as for a fixed-rate mortgage with monthly payments.

Words of Wisdom from Mortgage Consultant Mark Giordani

"A biweekly mortgage isn't much different than any other mortgage, except that the payments are made more often than once per month. What it boils down to is that if a mortgage payment is made biweekly, that's 26 payments per year, which equates to making 13 monthly payments per year instead of 12. I would not recommend paying extra for a biweekly payment privilege. If a broker or lender is going to charge you extra, consider accepting a traditional fixed-rate mortgage and then making one or more extra payments toward the loan's principal per year on your own. The result in terms of your savings will be basically the same and you will have control over when and whether or not to send in those extra payments."

More Mortgage Options for People with Less-Than-Perfect Credit

There is a wide range of mortgage options designed for people who have credit histories that are less than perfect or who don't have easily verifiable income. These people wouldn't typically qualify for a traditional, fixed-rate mortgage from a local bank or financial institution.

These mortgage options relate directly to what's required for loan approval and can be applied to a variety of mortgage products, although they're typically used for fixed-rate or adjustable-rate mortgages. As you'll discover, what's required to qualify will vary greatly by loan product and lender. These loans could have higher costs and higher interest rates than for a fixed-rate mortgage offered to someone with an excellent credit score. Be sure to discuss these options with your mortgage broker if you believe you could benefit from one of them in your financial situation. Some of these options are *subprime, non-conventional,* or *Alt-A* loans.

Dream Home Vocabulary

Stated-Income/Stated-Assets Mortgages—To qualify you for a mortgage, the lender will rely on financial information that you state is accurate, but you will not be required to furnish proof, such as tax returns, pay stubs, or bank statements.

Words of Wisdom from Mortgage Consultant Mark Giordani

"This type of loan is available to certain qualified borrowers on specific loan scenarios. The borrower does not need to provide any supporting documentation about their income or assets. The borrower literally just states what their income and assets are to the lender. This requires you to make a declaration to the lender that the information you're providing is totally accurate. Depending on your employment situation, requirements for this type of loan will vary. Keep in mind: a lender will verify your employment. If you state you're earning a specific salary for doing a specific job, the lender will also do research to make sure that the income you're declaring is within a reasonable and realistic range. Depending on the loan-to-value calculation and your credit situation, many lenders won't charge extra for this type of loan, nor will you have to pay a higher rate. A SISA (stated-income/stated-asset) loan can be a real timesaver."

Dream Home Vocabulary

No-Income-Verification Loans—To qualify for this type of mortgage product, the borrower will not need to provide proof of his or her income.

Words of Wisdom from Mortgage Consultant Mark Giordani

"This type of loan allows the borrower to potentially obtain a loan without having to state their income or prove their income. The approval decision is based primarily on assets owned and the borrower's credit. There are several different categories of no-income-verification loans. Again, as the risk for the lender increases, the rate the borrower will need to pay increases. These days, it is possible to obtain a mortgage without having to prove your income, assets, or employment, as long as you have qualifying credit."

Dream Home Vocabulary

No-Documentation Mortgages—To qualify for this type of loan, the borrower will need to have a qualifying credit history, but will not have to provide proof of income, assets, or employment.

Words of Wisdom from Mortgage Consultant Mark Giordani

"A lot of people assume that with this type of loan, there is no paperwork involved. That's not the case. There is still an application that needs to be completed. You will still need to provide your name, address, date of birth, Social Security number, and credit information. You will not, however, have to provide any information whatsoever about your assets, employment, or income. You may need to provide information about your current housing situation and how much you pay for rent. This may be verified later by the lender. A no-documentation loan means you don't need to supply a lot of supporting documents, like bank statements or pay stubs. There is still, however, a lot of paperwork involved with this type of loan during the closing itself.

"This type of loan is ideal for people who have privacy concerns and don't want to reveal certain information about their finances. For someone with poor credit and who desires a no-documentation loan, there's an entirely separate category of loans referred to as *hard-money loans*. Hard-money lenders primarily look at collateral or the value of the property, not at someone's credit or character. This type of lender typically won't lend more than 65 percent of the property's value. You'll also be required to pay a significantly higher interest rate and other fees."

Dream Home Vocabulary

No-Down-Payment Loans—For people who qualify, there are a variety of mortgage products that require either a very small or no down payment.

Words of Wisdom from Mortgage Consultant Mark Giordani

"A no-down-payment loan is one that requires absolutely no down payment. This is a 100-percent financed transaction, which has become extremely common these days. There are also loan programs that allow the borrower to receive a financial gift from a relative, for example, to cover their down payment. FHA loans and VA loans typically require little or no down payment. There are many loans that require only $500 of the borrower's own funds to use toward the home purchase. There are even loan programs that will provide the buyer with 103 percent of the property value, to help cover closing costs and other fees.

"On loans with no down payment or a down payment that's below 20 percent of the purchase price of the home, expect that in some circumstances you will be asked to pay for insurance for the lender in case the loan goes bad. This insurance is known as PMI or private mortgage insurance. There are many ways to get around this insurance requirement. Find a broker who is an expert in this area and you may be able to save some significant money."

Dream Home Vocabulary

Private Mortgage Insurance (MPI)—Borrowers applying for a conventional mortgage who don't have a 20-percent down payment are typically required to purchase *private mortgage insurance*, which is an insurance policy that guarantees the lender will be paid even if the borrower defaults on the loan. The cost of this insurance is paid by the borrower as an addition to the monthly mortgage payment. The lower the down payment, the higher the cost of this insurance. Once the borrower owns at least a 20-percent equity in his or her home, this insurance can be canceled and the mortgage can be adjusted accordingly.

FHA Loans

The Federal Housing Administration (FHA) offers government-insured loans that allow people to purchase property with low down payments. While the FHA is not a lender itself, it encourages lenders to offer loans to people who would otherwise not meet qualify for mortgages by guaranteeing the lender will be repaid, even if the borrower defaults. This is done by requiring the borrower to purchase special mortgage insurance (called a *mortgage insurance premium, MIP*). An estimate for the monthly cost of this added (required) insurance can be calculated by multiplying the loan amount by .5 and then dividing that number by 12. These MIP fees typically last for about seven years. MIP is similar to the private mortgage insurance (PMI) required for other types of loans.

Initially, FHA home loans were for first-time home buyers; however, they're not only for this purpose. Instead of requiring a 20-percent down payment, an FHA loan requires a down payment of three percent of the purchase price, which is much more affordable because the initial cash required to close the loan is lower.

There are preset loan limits for FHA loans that vary by region. To learn more, visit the FHA's web site at www.hud.gov or discuss this option with your mortgage broker.

Words of Wisdom from Mortgage Consultant Mark Giordani

"FHA loans are being insured by the Federal Housing Administration. Because the government is willing to bear some of the risk for the loans, lenders are willing to offer easier credit and income qualifications. These tend to be a little more complex and lengthier to apply for, because a number of government forms also need to be completed. Depending on the circumstances, this type of loan can save borrowers money. In other situations, however, the loan limits may not high enough to cover the purchase price of a home in certain geographic areas. A good mortgage broker will be able to help you determine if an FHA loan would be a better alternative than another type of loan and step you through the process."

Interest-Only Mortgage

In recent years, this has become a popular mortgage product among homebuyers, because it allows them to purchase a more expensive home without dramatically increasing their monthly payments. This type of loan is more suitable for people who expect their income to increase significantly in the future or who expect the value of their property to increase significantly over time.

As the name of this mortgage product suggests, the monthly payment represents only the interest due on the loan. No portion of the principal gets paid back each month. Thus, unless the property increases in value, no equity is ever built up. If the value of the property decreases before it's sold, the borrower could wind up owing money.

For this type of loan, a five- or ten-year interest-only period is standard. After this period, the principal is then amortized for the remaining term of the loan. Thus, if a borrower had a 30-year mortgage and paid interest only for the first ten years, at the end of that initial period, the principal would be amortized for the remaining 20 years. A borrower who expects his or her income to increase can borrow more than he or she could otherwise afford, because monthly payments are lower than for a typical fixed-rate mortgage.

Like all nontraditional mortgage products, this one has pros and cons that you should review with a financial planner or broker. Interest-only loans are not suitable for everyone.

Dream Home Tips

One common option is a more traditional type of loan that allows the borrower to make interest-only payments instead of full payments during months when money is tight. This gives homeowners an extra level of financial flexibility and the ability to better manage periodic unexpected expenses.

Words of Wisdom from Mortgage Consultant Mark Giordani

"Interest-only loans are a relatively new mortgage product. For the right borrower, they can be ideal. An interest-only loan has the potential to be riskier than other types of mortgages, but they also have many advantages, which you should discuss with your broker.

"This type of loan can be excellent if real estate prices are on the rise, because even though you're not building up equity in the home based on your monthly payments, you are building up equity if the value of the property increases. This type of loan is excellent for someone who doesn't have a steady income, who has a seasonal income, or who tends to be paid through on commissions. With this type of loan, the borrower always has the option to pay toward the principal of the loan and build equity at any time.

"If you utilize this type of loan, make sure you fully understand the terms. Interest-only loans are often associated with ARMs, as opposed to fixed-rate mortgages. There are, however, fixed-rate loans available that have an interest-only option, but expect to pay more in interest for this feature.

"One other advantage of an interest-only loan is something called 'recasting.'

If you take out a $200,000 fixed-rate loan, your monthly payment stays the same for the life of the loan—whether or not you pay any extra toward the principal balance.

With an interest-only loan, one nice feature is that if you are able to pay down the principal balance in an accelerated way, your monthly payments will reflect those payments, in most case, right away. So, as you are paying it down, your payments get lower. This can be a great feature for lots of borrowers who get their income in large payments or bonuses. With all loans, especially interest-only loans and ARMs, you must make every effort to understand what you are getting.

"If you take out a five-year interest-only loan, for example, your rate and payments would be fixed for five years. After the fifth year, however, your payment could go up if interest rates go up. Also, the entire principal balance of the loan will now have to be paid off over a 25-year payment schedule. This can mean sharp increases in the payments you need to make just a few years down the road.

"I would also suggest that first-time borrowers exercise caution with a new category of loans, called 'option loans,' 'pay option ARMs,' or 'pick-a-payment loans.' These loans traditionally offer three or four different monthly payment option scenarios. If used irresponsibly they can result in losing equity in your home. If you are offered a loan that features multiple payment options, including one payment option that doesn't even cover the monthly interest due, investgate fully."

VA Loans

The Department of Veterans Affairs (VA) offers mortgage opportunities to veterans of the U.S. military. This program has been in effect since 1944 and allows qualified borrowers to purchase a home with no down payment whatsoever. In other words, 100-percent financing is made available through this program. VA loans are available to enlisted service personnel with continuous service for a predetermined number of days (based on when the person served), a veteran with an honorable discharge, or a surviving spouse of an enlisted soldier killed in the line of duty. Some reservists also qualify. The amount that can be borrowed varies by region. These loans apply only to single- or multi-family home purchases that will be owner-occupied. Most VA loans are 15- or 30-year fixed-rate mortgages.

For additional information about VA loans, speak with a mortgage broker who specializes in this type of home financing option or visit the VA web site at www.homeloans.va.gov.

Words of Wisdom from Mortgage Consultant Mark Giordani

"Some VA loans are offered at very good rates and terms. They offer an excellent opportunity for veteran borrowers. The thing about VA loans is that there are not as many different mortgage product types available. In some cases, a non-VA loan may be better suited for a borrower. VA loans require extra paperwork and often take longer to process and get approved than other types of loans."

Assumable Loans

This is a mortgage that can be transferred from the seller of the home. The person taking over the loan assumes the liability for it and becomes responsible for making the monthly payments. This can be attractive if the seller has a very low interest rate for which you could not necessarily qualify. If you take over the seller's mortgage (assume his or her loan), you will be responsible for making a down payment of the difference between the balance owed on the loan and the selling price of the home .

Only mortgages that contain an *assumption clause* can be assumed. In most cases, ARM loans are assumable, while fixed-rate loans are not.

Words of Wisdom from Mortgage Consultant Mark Giordani

"Assumable loans aren't really an entirely separate type of loan, but are more of a feature that some loans include. The advantage is that if you sell the home, a new, qualified buyer may be able to take over the loan without having to refinance it. If an assumable loan is something that is extremely important to you, make sure the terms of the assumability are in writing and are exactly what you anticipated."

Some Pointers on Points

A point is equal to one percent of the mortgage amount. For a $100,000 loan, for example, one point would be $1,000. In order to reduce the interest rate offered on a loan, borrowers can often pay points on the loan at the closing. A one-point loan, for example, will have a lower interest rate than a zero-point loan. Points paid to reduce your interest rate are called *discount points*. Paying money at the closing as points means paying less money later in the form of interest. The money you pay for points is in addition to your down payment, not part of it.

In deciding whether or not to pay points on a loan, you should consider how long you plan to keep the property and whether or not you can recoup the amount you pay in points if you sell the property or refinance the loan within several years. As a general rule, it doesn't make sense to pay points on a loan if you plan on keeping that loan for less than four years.

Because lenders allow you to choose among rate-and-point combinations for the same loan product, the Mortgage101.com web site (www.mortgage101.com) recommends, "When comparing rates from different lenders, make sure you compare the associated points and rate combinations of the offered program. The published Annual Percentage Rate (APR) is a tool used to compare different terms, offered rates, and points among different lenders and programs."

It's important to note that some lenders charge points as part of their loan-origination fee.

Dream Home Vocabulary

Loan-to-value (LTV)—This is the ratio between the amount of the loan and the value of the property. Many types of mortgages have a specific LTV as a requirement for approval. If you're buying a home and making a 20-percent down payment, your LTV would be 80 percent. If you're making a five-percent down payment, your LTV would be 95 percent.

Dream Home Tips

If you're confused about the lingo used to describe various mortgage products, you're certainly not alone! Check out the mortgage glossary at the end of this book or the glossary found on the HUD web site (www.hud.gov/offices/hsg/sfh/buying/glossary.cfm). The Yahoo! Real Estate Glossary (realestate.yahoo.com/loans/glossary.html) is also a useful resource for decoding mortgage lingo.

Finding Your Dream Home

This chapter has provided you with basic knowledge you'll need for intelligent conversations with lenders and/or mortgage brokers about finding the perfect mortgage option to meet your financial needs. The next chapter offers advice on how to find your dream home and how to know when you've found it.

CHAPTER 4

Finding the Perfect Home

WHAT'S IN THIS CHAPTER

- Working with a real estate agent
- Alternative methods for finding your dream home
- Deciding where you'll live
- Considerations when choosing your dream home
- Determining your needs

Thus far, we've focused on some of the reasons why you might want to become a homeowner, reviewed how to prequalify or get preapproved for a mortgage, and learned about the various mortgage and financing options available to first-time prime and sub-prime borrowers. You have also learned about many of the steps involved in finding and buying a home.

Sure, this process can be confusing, but as you know, if you surround yourself with the right team of people—including an experienced and knowledgeable real estate agent, mortgage broker (or lender), real estate attorney, home inspector, and moving company—you'll discover this process can be extremely exciting and very manageable, even if you're also juggling a full-time job and family obligations.

This chapter focuses on how to decide where you should purchase your home and live, based on a wide range of considerations. You'll also discover some of the many benefits to working with a Realtor® to help you navigate your way through the often confusing home-buying process.

Dream Home Tips

As you'll learn later in this chapter, there's a difference between a licensed real estate agent and a Realtor®. When choosing the person with whom you'll work, understand that fees are negotiable and that the services offered vary greatly. Finding the right person—someone who is experienced and knowledgeable and who understands your needs—can save you time, money, and a lot of hassle.

Before you begin searching for your dream home, do research to determine:

- What you can afford
- Where you'd like to live
- What the current real estate market is like
- What the current mortgage rates are that you qualify for
- What your current and future needs for a home
- What you consider your ideal home to be like in size and style

If you decide to work with a full-service real estate agent, that person will help you analyze your individual or family needs and serve as your guide as you explore communities and visit homes. The Internet is also an extremely powerful tool for doing research, whether you're planning to move across town, to a neighboring state, or across the country.

Dream Home Tips

Plan on allowing between 30 and 40 days for conducting a comprehensive search for a suitable home. During this time, you'll probably evaluate and tour from 20 to 40 homes. Ideally, this is a process that should not be rushed. You're more apt to find the perfect home if you invest the necessary time to do research or work with a qualified real estate agent. However, if you're in a time crunch and must find a home and move in under a month, this is possible, but it will increase considerably the pressure and stress, especially if you're looking to find your dream home.

Working with a Real Estate Agent

If you're thinking about moving to another community and want to learn more about where you hope to move; if you need help finding the perfect house; if you require assistance in defining your needs and analyzing your financial situation; if you want referrals for a mortgage broker, an attorney, a home inspector, and/or a title company; and if you would benefit from assistance when negotiating with the seller once you find the ideal property, then a real estate agent who represents you—the buyer—can be a tremendous help.

A full-service real estate agent who specializes in the geographic area where you'd like to move will know everything there is to know about that community, be very familiar with the properties currently on the market, have a thorough understanding of the current real estate market, and have the knowledge and experience to help you through it the entire process.

The next section of this chapter features an in-depth interview with Thomas Stevens, president of the National Association of Realtors®. From him, you'll learn there are more than 2.5 million licensed real estate agents in America. In virtually every town, city, or community across the country, you'll be able to find a knowledgeable, experienced, and reliable real estate agent to help you find and purchase your dream home. You just need to choose the right person.

It's important to understand that a real estate agent can represent either the buyer or the seller and that the agent will earn from four to six percent of the home's selling price as a commission for his or her services. These fees, however, are negotiable. It's not necessary to have a real estate agent represent you—but it's definitely recommended if this is the first home you're buying!

An agent who represents the seller is obligated to work on behalf of the seller to market the home, seek out qualified buyers, and get the potential buyers to offer the highest amount possible for the property. The seller's agent can pass along to the seller any information provided by a potential buyer, which can put that buyer at a disadvantage when negotiating the sale price for the property. For example, if you tell a seller's agent about your budget, the down payment you can afford, and/or the size of the mortgage for which you're prequalified or preapproved, that agent now knows exactly how much you're able to spend. There may be no reason for him or her negotiate a lower selling price with you. If the real estate agent represents you, the buyer, he or she must keep your personal financial information confidential.

The residential real estate business is highly competitive. You should choose someone who understands your needs, who will work around your schedule, and who is both knowledgeable and experienced.

Here are some of the best ways to find the ideal real estate agent:

- Obtain a referral from a friend, relative, or co-worker who has had a positive experience working with a specific real estate agent.

- Obtain a referral from a lender, mortgage broker, real estate attorney, financial planner, CPA, home inspector, or someone else who works in the real estate industry and who can provide an unbiased referral.
- Visit the Realtor.com web site's free referral service (www.realtor.com/FindReal).
- Respond to ads in local newspapers or the Yellow Pages in the area where you're planning to move.
- Visit web sites hosted by real estate agents. (Use a search engine, such as Yahoo! or Google, and enter the search phrase, "real estate agent, Peoria, Illinois" or "Realtor, Boston, Massachusetts" for example.)

Once you decide to work with a real estate agent, he or she should give you an *agency disclosure* document that outlines the relationship between you and that person. (This is required in most states.) This document should clearly state whether or not this person represents you, what their fees will be, and how those fees will be paid.

Dream Home Vocabulary

Agency Disclosure Document—This document will be provided by the real estate agent you choose. It describes which party they represent (the buyer or the seller), how they're compensated, which services are offered, and the overall terms of the relationship. You and that person should sign it.

Dream Home Tips

Before choosing a real estate agent, interview him or her. Learn about his or her experience, knowledge, and familiarity with the community where you want to move. Determine if that person will represent you, the buyer and if he or she is a licensed Realtor® or a licensed real estate agent. (You'll learn the difference shortly.)

Working with a real estate agent who represents you provides several advantages. Right from the start, you can take full advantage of his or her experience and knowledge about the community where you hope to move. This includes learning about current real estate values, taxes, utility costs, municipal services, and local schools. Without doing too much research on your own, you can also learn about current market conditions and discover which properties are available that best meet your needs. Ultimately, an experienced real estate agent who represents you will also help you negotiate with the seller and potentially save you money.

The real estate agent you choose must be licensed in the state in which he or she works, either as an agent, a salesperson, or a broker. To obtain this license, a person must complete state-specific educational requirements, successfully pass an exam, and be issued a license.

☆ ☆ **WARNING** ☆ ☆

Only licensed real estate agents who are members in good standing of the National Association of Realtors® can promote themselves as Realtors®. This means they've agreed to adhere to a strict code of ethics developed by the association.

Once you hire a real estate agent to represent you, you can expect that person to put your interests first in the home-buying process. This includes keeping any and all personal or financial information you provide confidential and following your instructions when dealing with potential sellers.

TIP: When you start looking at many homes, it will be difficult to keep track of them. A good strategy is to carry a digital (or even disposable) camera and a notebook, so you can take photos and notes about the homes as you see them. Before beginning your home search, create a checklist for yourself, like the one that follows. Lists the main features you want in a home. As you tour each home, mark down the pros and cons of that property and any notes that'll help you remember it better.

Creating a Home Tour Checklist

Before your home search begins, develop a checklist that lists all of the features you want in a home. As you tour each home, use this checklist to help you evaluate whether the property could be your dream home.

Dream Home Tips

As you develop a checklist that describes all of the features of your dream home, look through real estate and home décor magazines for ideas.

The following is a sample generic checklist. You'll want to develop a checklist for yourself that lists features that you want and need.

A Sample Home Tour Checklist

- ❑ Appropriate number of bedrooms for current and future needs
- ❑ Good bedroom sizes with ample closet space in each
- ❑ Bright living room with large windows
- ❑ Fireplace
- ❑ Hardwood floors
- ❑ Wall-to-wall carpeting in the bedrooms
- ❑ Fully equipped kitchen
- ❑ Finished basement
- ❑ Attic or basement for storage
- ❑ Laundry room in a convenient location
- ❑ Space for a home office
- ❑ Adequate number of full and half bathrooms
- ❑ Whirlpool tub in the master bath
- ❑ Rooms wired for cable TV and high-speed Internet
- ❑ Space for a nursery and separate playroom
- ❑ Two-car garage
- ❑ Roof, electrical, plumbing, air conditioning, heating, and hot water systems all in good working condition
- ❑ In a good community
- ❑ On a quiet street
- ❑ In a safe community
- ❑ Real estate taxes affordable
- ❑ Ready to occupy with little or no repair or renovation work required

Questions to Ask a Real Estate Agent

Just as you'd hire a qualified accountant or CPA to help you with a tax problem or a good attorney to help you with an important legal matter, working with an experienced and knowledgeable real estate agent is an optional, but important step in the home-buying process—especially for first-time buyers.

Before hiring someone, consider asking these questions during your initial meeting or phone consultation:

- Do you have an active real estate license in good standing?
- Do you belong to a Multiple Listing Service and have access to most or all of the best listings in the area?
- Is working as a Realtor® or real estate agent your full-time career? How long have you been doing it?
- Will you be representing me or the seller? (Every state has its own guidelines for the responsibilities entailed in representation, so make sure you understand his or her legal obligations to you and to the seller.)
- Can you describe the process of finding and purchasing a home? How will you be involved? What services and benefits will you offer during each phase of the process?
- What are your fees? How will you be compensated? Can we negotiate these fees in advance?
- What is your availability? Will you be able to work with me in the evenings and on weekends, based on my work schedule?

☆ ☆ **WARNING** ☆ ☆

If you're dealing directly with a seller's agent, don't reveal your confidential financial information to that person. He or she will most likely share it with the seller, putting you at a disadvantage during your negotiations.negative financial situation you experience in the future.

Dream Home Vocabulary

Multiple Listing Service (MLS)—MLS is a network of online databases containing home and property listings. It is accessible to licensed real estate agents and brokers (and in many cases their clients); virtually all agents and brokers are members of MLS or have access to the databases. MLS allows agents to view details about homes represented by other agents. This service typically does not permit listings for properties that are for sale by owner. As a home buyer, you can access MLS listings through various real estate web sites, several are which are described in this chapter.

Meet Thomas Stevens, President, National Association of Realtors®

Thomas Stevens is president of the National Association of Realtors® (www.realtor.com), a professional association founded in 1908 that now has more than one million members worldwide. The term "Realtor" refers exclusively to members who are not only licensed real estate agents, but also adhere to the strict membership guidelines and a stringent code of ethics enforced by the association. It's important to understand that not all licensed real estate agents are Realtors®, but all Realtors® are licensed real estate agents.

In this interview, Tom, who has 34 years experience working as a Realtor®, discusses how to find the perfect Realtor® when purchasing a home, the difference between an agent who represents the buyer and an agent who represents the seller, and what services a buyer can expect from his or her Realtor®.

Dream Home Tips

To learn more about The National Association of Realtors®, find a qualified Realtor® in your region to work with, or use the free home-buying information and tools available from this association, visit www.realtor.com or www.realtor.org.

What exactly is the National Association of Realtors®?

Tom Stevens: "The National Association is the largest professional association in America, with over 1.2 million members. What we do is provide support, training, and a code of ethics that our Realtors® subscribe to. We also provide a vast amount of information to consumers through our web sites."

What is the difference between a real estate agent and a Realtor®?

Tom Stevens: "There are over 2.5 million licensed real estate agents in America. The 1.2 million Realtors® are the people who are fully licensed, but who also follow the guidelines and code of ethics established by our association. This code of ethics focuses on the fiduciary responsibility Realtors® have to their clients."

How should a first-time home buyer go about finding a good Realtor®?

Tom Stevens: "One of the first things I recommend is seeking out a referral from someone you know and trust. Most people have had firsthand experience working with a Realtor® or know someone who has. You'll probably be more confident in your selection if someone you know has already had a good experience working with that person. If nobody you know can recommend a Realtor®, call your local Association of Realtors® or visit the Realtor.com web site to obtain a free referral. In addition to finding a referral from our web site, you'll also be able to access information about more than 95 percent of the properties currently available in the United States. I recommend finding an agent who is extremely familiar with the area you're interested in moving into."

What are some of the questions a home buyer should ask a Realtor® or real estate agent *before* hiring him or her?

Tom Stevens: "In addition to making sure they know the area where you want to move, I suggest asking about their experience and how long they've been working in real estate. Determine if the agent knows and understands the current real estate market. One of the most important questions to ask is whether or not the person is a full-service agent or

Realtor®. Ask specifically what services they provide. Does the Realtor® know the key mortgage brokers in the area? Do they have access to all of the listings in the marketplace? Does the Realtor® have a relationship with a title company to help with the closing? You want to hire someone who can recommend whom to hire for all of the services you'll ultimately need. Ask the Realtor® to explain the current real estate market to you for the area where you want to live. Determine if the person has an understanding of your needs after you've explained your basic situation and goals in terms of what type of home you're looking for. If the quality of the schools is important to your family, for example, make sure the Realtor® knows about the school system and will be able to answer your questions, while also addressing your concerns."

How much research should a home buyer do in advance of working with a Realtor®?

Tom Stevens: "The Realtor® you hire will be able to help you find the perfect home, based on your needs. However, you'll need to describe those needs to the person you decide to work with. Are you part of a growing family or is your family downsizing? It's important to know what your current and future needs are, so the Realtor® can help address them. I would recommend that you develop a basic understanding of the home-buying process, your financial situation, and what the real estate market is like before starting your home search."

What does a home buyer need to know about the fees a Realtor® will charge?

Tom Stevens: "First, fees are negotiable. It's important to develop an understanding right away with the Realtor® you'll be working with, so you know exactly what services are offered and what the fees are. If you're looking to hire a full-service Realtor®, expect to pay a commission equal to five, six, or even seven percent of the home's purchase price. Typically, this commission will be split between the buyer and seller. Most properties that are listed in the Multiple Listing Service, for example, already incorporate the commission to be paid to the Realtor®."

What is an *agency agreement* that a home buyer will be expected to sign with a Realtor®?

Tom Stevens: "Most buyers sign an agency agreement that states that the Realtor® or real estate agent is representing them, even if the commission is being paid by the seller. As the buyer, it's important to have a real estate agent or Realtor® representing you, as opposed to the seller. This will ensure that your interests are being met. If a Realtor® does not meet the requirements of the agreement you both sign, a complaint can be filed and their license could be taken away."

From the buyer's perspective, what's the difference whether the Realtor® represents them or the seller?

Tom Stevens: "There is a huge difference. If I list a property and a seller has hired me to represent them, as the Realtor®, my job is to get them their asking price or higher for the property from the buyer. My responsibility is to protect the seller's interests and get them the highest price possible. If I am representing the buyer, my fiduciary responsibility is to that buyer. I know what their needs are. The buyer has confided in me about their finances, and I cannot disclose this information to the seller. I know how much money they have available to make a purchase and my job is to help the buyer negotiate the best possible price. If a home buyer is represented by a Realtor®, there's a good chance they'll ultimately save money when purchasing their home. A Realtor® can also help prevent costly problems, delays, and mistakes during the home-buying process."

Dream Home Tips

It's important to understand that while a Realtor® may have strong business relationships with mortgage brokers, real estate attorneys, title companies, or home inspectors, it is against the law for him or her to receive a kickback from the service provider for providing a referral. "In most cases," says Tom Stevens, president of the National Association of Realtors®, "the Realtor® will be able to offer you several referrals based on positive past experiences their clients have had. A home buyer should feel comfortable utilizing referrals from their Realtor® and consider them reliable."

What are some of the biggest misconceptions home buyers have about what a Realtor® is and what services they offer?

Tom Stevens: "One misconception is that fees are not negotiable and that all fees are preset. This isn't the case when it comes to working with a real estate agent or Realtor®. When discussing fees, make sure you understand exactly what services are being offered, what's included in the fee, and who the Realtor® will represent—the buyer or the seller. The agent is supposed to disclose who they are working for and are loyal to."

What are some of the common mistakes first-time home buyers make with a Realtor® or real estate agent?

Tom Stevens: "The biggest mistake I see made often is that the buyer doesn't commit to one Realtor®. They jump around. Once you find a Realtor® or real estate agent to work with, whom you feel is capable of helping you, stick with that person. Keep in mind that Realtors® specialize in different markets. You'll have a much easier time if you develop one relationship with a single Realtor®.

"Another mistake I've seen people make is that they rush their home-buying decision. Often, if you take your time looking for the perfect home and take the time to negotiate the best price, you'll feel more comfortable with your purchase and you'll reduce your chances of experiencing buyer's remorse. You should never be forced or pushed into a home-buying decision.

"Always hire a home inspector to inspect the home before purchasing it. This will help you understand what work needs to be done on the home before it is too late. You want to know, in advance, if the roof, plumbing, electrical system, septic system, or any of the major appliances, for example, are in disrepair or will need to be replaced in the near future. You want to know if the home has a termite problem or any other problems that will need to be addressed, before it becomes your problem and your expense."

How much time should a home buyer plan to invest in order to find the perfect home and how many homes should they plan on looking at?

Tom Stevens: "Once you explain to the Realtor® what you're looking for, the time it takes to find the perfect home could be anywhere from a few days to 30 days or longer. It's average for someone to look at between 15 and 25 properties before making an offer on one. If you're coming to town and need to find a home in one week, chances are you'll find one. If you're moving across town and have the luxury of taking your time, taking between 30 and 60 days to find a home is normal."

Is there a good time of year to begin searching for a home to buy?

Tom Stevens: "Spring is always an excellent time of year to begin your new home search, because inventory is always at its highest and you'll probably have a greater selection to choose from. When more properties are available for sale, there's more competition and it's easier for the buyer to negotiate a better deal."

After choosing a Realtor®, what's the next step for the buyer?

Tom Stevens: "If the Realtor® will be representing you, the buyer, one of the first things you'll want to do is sit down with the Realtor® for a qualifying meeting. During this meeting, the Realtor® will go over your finances, wants, needs, and concerns and help you define exactly what you're looking for and are capable of purchasing based on your finances. Be prepared to discuss your finances, debts, income, and credit history. The more information you provide about your goals, the easier it will be for the Realtor® to help you find a property that meets those goals. A good Realtor® will also help you plan for your needs in the future."

Is it acceptable to expect your Realtor® to be available evenings, nights, and weekends to work around your schedule?

Tom Stevens: "Yes, but within reason. A Realtor® understands you have a job and family responsibilities, so they'll make themselves available to work with you when you can spare the time. Keep in mind, however, that Realtors® also have personal lives. If you have specific scheduling needs, discuss this early on with the Realtor® you choose to work with to ensure those needs can be accommodated. Most Realtors® are readily available evenings and weekends as they're needed. Realtors® provide a tremendous amount of service to their clients and can help look out for your interests and save you money. A Realtor's® job is to sell the American dream. They work hard for their fees and if they're a Realtor®, as opposed to a real estate agent, you can have faith that they're reputable."

Alternative Methods for Finding Your Dream Home

A real estate agent will be able to help you identify the best available properties in the area you'd like to move. It's their job to stay up-to-date on listings and know what's available. If you choose not to work with a real estate agent, you can do much of this research yourself using the following methods:

- Review the real estate section of the local newspaper or regional magazines.
- Attend open houses hosted by sellers.
- Drive through a neighborhood looking for "For Sale" signs.
- Conduct an Internet search for current property listings.
- Learn about properties for sale through word-of-mouth from friends, relatives, and co-workers.

Each of these methods requires a time investment on your part, to do the research that a real estate agent would have done for you.

Real Estate Web Sites Worth Checking Out

If you have access to the Internet, you already know it's an extremely powerful tool. It can make finding your dream home as easy as conducting an online search using real estate web sites. There are thousands of web sites that offer current property listings across the country, available 24 hours a day, seven days a week. So, you can do your research when it's convenient.

In addition to the two web sites operated by the National Association of Realtors® (www.realtor.com and www.realtor.org), the following list of real estate web sites will be extremely useful, helping you do the following:

- Research the current real estate market and home prices.
- Find a real estate agent.
- Get answers to your real estate questions.
- Learn about geographic areas and communities where you might be interested in living.
- View detailed available property listings by city, town, state, or ZIP code.

Century 21 Real Estate

www.century21.com

Most people know Century 21 as the world's largest residential real estate sales organization, with more than 6,600 independently owned and operated franchised broker offices in over 30 countries and territories worldwide. The company's web site is designed to be a "one-stop shop" for home buyers. You can review property listings, find a Century 21 agent, learn about financing options, view current mortgage rates, and access the company's free online home buyer's guide.

The web site gives home buyers access to properties listed with Century 21 offices and properties listed with the Multiple Listing Service (MLS). You can search listings by city, state, or ZIP code, as well as by search radius, price range, number of bedrooms, and/or number of bathrooms. Within seconds, you'll get an abbreviated listing of properties available. You can then click on the "Details" icon to learn more about a property and obtain contact information for the local Century 21 agent who represents it. After choosing one or more properties of interest, click on the "Map" icon to see the location of each property.

This is an extremely user-friendly site that provides a wealth of valuable information to home buyers. Even if you don't use a Century 21 agent, you can learn a lot from visiting this web site and using its free online tools.

Homes.com

www.homes.com

This web site is owned and operated by Trader Publishing Company, a provider of "media to bring buyers and sellers together."

From the Homes.com web site, a home buyer can access a

wide range of free online services, including:

6 BULLETS

- Information on neighborhoods and local real estate conditions for any area
- Nationwide property listings in a database of more than one million homes
- Referrals for Realtors® and real estate agents
- Advice on moving
- Articles and news stories about real estate and the current market
- Real estate and financial calculators

This web site also allows searches of online property listings for new homes or foreclosures. You can also download listings of interest to your Palm or Pocket PC personal digital assistant.

Move.com

www.move.com

This web site taps into a vast amount of information from other real estate web sites (including realtor.com) to provide a comprehensive set of online tools for home buyers. It allows them to search through millions of nationwide property listings in minutes and define their search criteria to identify only the most appropriate listings.

Move.com also offers online tools for helping you determine how much you can afford, research mortgage rates, obtain details about local public and private schools, find a mover, and obtain a referral for a Realtor® or real estate agent. The site also provides information, articles, and advice about moving and settling into your new home and community.

Moving.com

www.moving.com

Once you've purchased your home, this web site will help you plan and execute your move. The site features a wide range of articles, tools, and referrals for moving companies, moving supply companies, truck rental services, and more. You can also find local self-storage facilities and utility providers and learn about homeowner's insurance. Whether you're moving across town or across the country, this web site is an excellent resource that could save you time, aggravation, and money. (Be sure to read Chapter 8 for more information about planning your move.)

Prudential Real Estate

www.prudential.com/realestate

This web site is designed to provide home buyers with a comprehensive set of online tools and information, including nationwide property listings. Prudential Real Estate brokerage services are offered through the network of offices that are independently owned and operated.

In addition to allowing access to millions of current property listings, this web site allows home buyers to research specific communities and access a free, online home buyer's guide. Upon reviewing listings, visitors to this web site can obtain a referral to a local Prudential Real Estate Realtor®, broker, or agent.

RE/MAX

www.remax.com

RE/MAX is "a global real estate system of franchisee-owned and -operated offices and their affiliated independent professionals." The company's web site is designed to provide a vast amount of information and powerful tools for prospective home buyers. While this web site doesn't offer the same advanced property listing search tools as other real estate sites, it offers a wide range of information, including a detailed first-time home buyer's guide. As you'd expect, with a few clicks of the mouse, you can locate a RE/MAX real estate agent to help you with your home-buying needs.

RealEstate.com

www.realestate.com

In addition to offering quick access to millions of real estate listings nationwide, RealEstate.com (a service of LendingTree) provides a complete set of tools, tips, calculators, and resources that you can use as you progress throughout the home-buying process. You can view property listings, find a Realtor®, access home-buying guides, and learn about financing options. You can also find referrals for insurance brokers, moving companies, home inspectors, local utility companies, and a range of other services.

Yahoo! Real Estate

realestate.yahoo.com

In addition to being one of the most powerful and popular Internet directories and search engines in the world, Yahoo! can help with real estate. This site is designed to provide easy access to a wide range of information and services for home buyers. You can follow links to property listings, referrals for real estate agents, read online home-buying guides, and use financial tools and calculators. The only drawback to this web site is the abundance of display ads and sponsored links on each page.

Zillow.com

www.zillow.com

If you're interested in the value of virtually any home in America, this web site can provide this information in seconds. Simply type in the full address of the property and its value will be displayed in seconds, along with information about neighboring properties—usually with a bird's-eye view of the location through aerial and satellite photography.

You should use this information only as an approximation, as accuracy varies based on various factors. Be sure to read the "How to use Zillow" section of the web site to determine how you can and should use the information it provides.

Zillow.com enables you to compare home prices within a community. This information will help you when making an offer and negotiating with a seller. You can also review information about recently sold homes in any area and easily compare neighboring home values with the seller's asking price.

Not only is Zillow.com extremely useful and easy to use, it makes doing real estate research fun. Once you've found some homes or communities of interest, you can learn more about them immediately.

Deciding Where You'll Live

Now that you've decided to become a home owner and you've taken the preliminary financial steps with a lender or mortgage broker to get prequalified or preapproved, the next step is deciding where you'd like to live and what type of home you'd like to purchase. Single-family homes come in all styles, shapes, colors, and sizes. There are also multi-family homes, apartments, and condos. The type of home should relate directly to your needs and fit your finances.

And where do you want to find your dream home? Is there a specific town, city, or community where you're interested in looking? Can you afford to live in that location? Is it convenient to where you work? How close is the home to shopping, schools, and/or public transportation, for example? Just as you've identified what you want and need in a home, think about what you're looking for in a community. Are you a city dweller or someone who prefers the suburbs?

Would you prefer a single-family home with a large lawn or a condominium where all of the yard work is handled for you?

As you begin thinking about where you'd like to live, first focus on a state or a city and then narrow down your search to a few towns or communities in that state or to areas within that city. Next, research those areas and calculate the cost of living there. Also, research the current real estate market in those areas to make sure you can afford to live there and purchase a home that'll meet your needs.

If you've decided you must live within a certain area because it's close to your work and you don't want a long commute, investigate communities within five or ten miles of that area. You'll often find that real estate prices can vary greatly if you move just a few blocks within a city or to a nearby community.

In addition to reviewing home prices, think about real estate taxes and insurance costs, which will also vary greatly by area. Consider also any commuting costs, including parking (if applicable), and/or condo/homeowners' association fees (if applicable). Your real estate agent will be able to help you focus on areas to live, based on your preferences, needs, and financial situation.

Dream Home Tips

You may need to make concessions during the home search process. For example, you may find the ideal home in the ideal community, but realize it would be a 30-minute commute to and from work. Or, to be near work, you may have to settle on a home with a smaller lawn or without the extra-large bedrooms you were hoping for. Keep an open mind, even after you decide on exactly the type of home and community.

Other Things to Consider When Choosing Your Dream Home

After selecting a city, town, or community where you'd like to live, consider the following factors as you evaluate properties:

- **Climate**—How important is the weather to you and your lifestyle? You can learn about the climate in any part of the country by visiting the Weather.com web site (www.weather.com).
- **Commute to and from Work**—How would your commute to and from work be? How long? How is the traffic? What would the commute cost in terms of fuel, tolls, parking, and bus fare and/or train fare each month? Be sure to calculate commuting costs into your monthly budget.
- **Financial Considerations**—Can you afford the home itself, along with the taxes, insurance, and upkeep?
- **Future Plans**—Are you planning to grow your family? Will you need additional bedrooms? In a few years, will your kids be going off to school or moving out? What will your needs be in three, five, or ten years? How long do you plan to stay in this home?
- **Homeowners' Association Bylaws (Rules and Regulations)**—Many housing complexes and virtually all condominium and apartment complexes have strict

bylaws. These are rules and regulations for residents. Read any rules carefully and make sure you would have no trouble following them, before you decide to buy the property.

- **Location**—Is the home convenient to shopping, public transportation, schools, or other places you'll be visiting often?
- **Parking**—If you own or lease a car, think about the parking situation near the home. Consider convenience as well as cost. In addition to thinking about where you'll park your own car(s) and any costs, think about parking for guests. Are there laws regulating on-street parking near the home?
- **Potential Neighbors**—Living close to other people can be wonderful if you get along with your neighbors. If, however, you don't get along with your neighbors, the stress and frustration can make your situation unpleasant. Try to learn as much as possible about the neighbors before purchasing a home. Hopefully the people you'll be living near will have a lifestyle similar to yours or at least compatible. For example, if you have school-age children, you might not want to live next to a grumpy old couple that hates children and noise.
- **Quality of the Schools**—If you have school-age children, the location and quality of the schools may be extremely important to you. Your real estate agent will most likely be able to provide information about the

school system. However, you could also call the school or speak with other parents in the area.

You can obtain free information about school systems anywhere in the United States from the Yahoo! School Reports web site (realestate.yahoo.com/re/schools). These reports give the number of students enrolled, student-to-teacher ratio, average class size, graduation rates, etc. Another excellent resource for learning about schools is the American School Directory (www.asd.com).

- **Real Estate Market**—Research the current real estate market. Do you anticipate home prices dropping in the near future or do you believe they'll rise over time? One of the worst mistakes you can make is planning to live in a home for a just a few years, building up very little equity, and then, when you're ready to sell, realizing that home prices have dropped. You could lose money and wind up upside-down on your mortgage. (This is when the value of a home is less than what is owed on the mortgage.) You'd then have to pay the difference if you sell. Working with a real estate agent and a financial planner as you buy your home and carefully analyzing your long-term needs can help you avoid this all-too-common problem.
- **Real Estate Taxes**—Local property taxes are based on the value of your property and vary greatly from community to community. Calculate real estate taxes into your budget. This expense is critical. Failing to pay real

estate taxes when they're due will result in hefty fines. Failing to pay real estate taxes altogether will result in a lien on your home and can lead to costly legal problems or worse. To learn about local taxes, you can visit the web site for the local government, which you can find through www.firstgov.gov.

- **Safety of the Neighborhood**—Check the crime rate in the area and determine if the community is safe. Will you need to install an alarm system, security bars, and extra locks on the doors and windows? Will you be able to walk your dog alone at night safely? Will your children be safe playing in the area or at the local park? Safety is an important consideration when choosing a home.
- **Standard of Living**—Compare the difference in the cost of living between where you live now and where you hope to live. Use a free Standard of Living calculator on one of these web sites: www.homefair.com/homefair/calc/salcalc.html or salary.monster.com/CostOfLivingWizard/layoutscripts/coll_start.asp.

In addition to all of these considerations, think about your own situation, lifestyle, and living habits to determine if where you're planning to move is suitable or if you'll be required to make serious concessions or sacrifices. If so, are you willing to make them? Once you define your needs, with ample research and working with a qualified real estate agent, you should be able to find a home you can afford that meets your needs. If, for whatever reason, you're not finding exactly what you're looking for, consider the concessions you're willing to make, think about broadening your geographic search, or consider working with a different agent who may know the local market better.

Determining Your Personal Needs

One of the biggest wastes of time and energy in searching for the perfect home is touring properties that are in no way what you want and need. To avoid this problem, first define what you want and need in a living situation as succinctly and accurately as possible and then determine what you can afford. Make sure you communicate this information to your real estate agent. Once the agent has a good feel for your personal tastes, needs, and finances, he or she can better choose which available properties to show you.

Ask yourself these questions as you define your personal needs:

- What do you need in a home? Consider size, number of bedrooms, number of bathrooms, size of the kitchen, size of the lawn, amenities, and so on.
- Where do you want to live? How important is the location?
- What kind of home do you want? Single-family, multi-family, condominium, apartment? What style? Is the age of the home important?
- What type of community would you like to live in?

Dream Home Tips

To learn more about a community, read its newspaper. You can find the local newspaper and determine if there's an online edition by visiting the Newspapers.com web site (www.newspapers.com).

You've Found Your Dream Home—Now What?

Finding the perfect place to live might take days, weeks, or months. Once you find that place, the next step is to make an offer on the property and begin negotiating with the seller. The next chapter focuses on how to approach a seller and make an offer, whether or not you're working with a real estate agent.

CHAPTER 5

Making an Offer on Your Dream Home

WHAT'S IN THIS CHAPTER

- Discovering the value of the home you like
- Evaluating the seller's asking price
- Making a formal offer to the seller
- Getting the home inspected
- Tips from a home inspector
- Negotiating your best price

Thus far, you've figured out your finances and learned how to get prequalified or preapproved for a mortgage, learned about the types of mortgage products available to first-time home buyers, learned about the steps involved in the home-buying process, and discovered strategies for finding your dream home. This chapter focuses on the steps to take once you've found the perfect home you want to buy.

Discovering the Value of the Home

Once you've found what you believe to be the home you'd like to own, the next step is to do some research about the home, community, and current real estate market. The more you know about the home's history, any repairs or renovation it might need, the state of the local economy, and recent selling prices of similar homes in the area, the better off you'll be when you're making an offer and negotiating the best price possible for that property.

Your real estate agent will help you conduct the necessary research and assist you in this important phase of the home-buying process. Remember: if you're working with a real estate agent, he or she must be working on your behalf, not on behalf of the seller. By this step, you should already have an agreement in writing that outlines the relationship between you and your agent.

Before making an offer on a property, you want to know its appraised value, its current market value, and the seller's asking price. These three numbers may be very similar or dramatically different, depending on the situation. For example, if the real estate market in that community is booming and there is a huge demand for homes and lots of potential, qualified buyers, the asking price for the home could be significantly higher than its appraised value. Yet you don't want to pay far too much for a home based on what similar homes in the neighborhood have recently sold for in similar market conditions.

In addition to reviewing the home's appraised value, its current market value, and the asking price, one excellent resource for learning about a home's value is the Zillow.com web site (www.zillow.com), described in Chapter 4. Also, consider the value of the home to you in terms of location, features, condition, community, and anything else that's important to you. Are you willing to pay a premium to live closer to your work or public transportation? After purchasing the home, will you have to invest a significant amount of money in renovations or major repairs? These are just some of the things to consider before making your initial offer on the property.

Make a Formal Offer to the Seller

As soon as you find the perfect home, consider making an offer on it as quickly as possible to ensure that it won't be sold to someone else. However, make sure adequate contingencies are put into your offer to protect your interests and allow you to withdraw the offer (with no financial penalty) if the seller doesn't meet specific requirements.

Dream Home Vocabulary

Offer—An offer on a home is a formal bid to buy it. This should be done through a real estate agent, but it can be done independently. Making an offer involves putting together a written bid, which will include details such as the address of the home, the bid for the property, the type of financing to be used to purchase the home, and a target date for closing and occupancy. It should also list contingencies that must be met for the offer to be binding. A financial deposit may be required in conjunction with the offer; depending on the situation, this deposit may or may not be refundable. Offers should always be in writing, by verbal agreement between the buyer and the seller or the seller's agent or other representative.

Once you make an offer, if all of the contingencies are met, the seller accepts your offer, and you haven't withdrawn it before the expiration or rescission date, that offer becomes a legally binding agreement to purchase the home.

Dream Home Vocabulary

Contingencies—Your written offer should include contingencies that protect your interests. A contingency requires that specified criteria be met in order for the contract to take effect. For example, the offer can be contingent on completion of a satisfactory home inspection, determination that the seller has a clear title to the home, approval of the buyer's financing, and completion of specific repairs on the home prior to closing. Your agent can help you develop a list of contingencies appropriate for your situation.

Remember: the seller wants to sell his or her home for the highest price possible and do the least little repair work possible on the property. Your objective is to purchase the home

One contingency you'll want to include is that the lender must fully approve your mortgage or you have the right to withdraw your offer.

Dream Home Tips

for the lowest price possible and ensure that it's in pristine move-in condition in time for the closing. The conflicting wishes of buyer and seller often cause disagreements during the negotiating process. An experienced and qualified agent representing you can make this process much easier and protect your interests throughout the process.

The seller may choose to accept your offer or may choose not to accept it but make a counteroffer with a different asking price. At this point, you and the seller (or your agents) will begin a formal negotiation.

Making an intelligent offer can be tricky. If you offer too little (less than the asking price), you run a good chance that the seller will reject your offer. You also run the risk that another buyer will come along and make a more attractive offer. If you offer too much, you could wind up wasting your money, especially if the asking price on the home was already inflated.

The seller might reject your offer not because of the price, but because of your proposed closing date and/or move-in date or because of a disagreement with one or more of the contingencies in the offer. If your offer gets rejected, determine exactly why and then act accordingly. It isn't always necessary offer more money. The seller may simply want to push back the closing date and/or the move-in date by a few weeks to accommodate his or her schedule.

If your initial offer gets rejected, the seller may make a counteroffer or expect you to make a counteroffer. Figure out what's expected and act accordingly. If the seller makes a counteroffer, it's up to you to accept it or to reject it and then potentially make another counteroffer. This back-and-forth can go several rounds until the price and the terms are acceptable to both buyer and seller. Again, your real estate agent should be guide you through this process, help you prepare your offer(s) and counteroffer(s), and help you evaluate counteroffers by the seller.

Dream Home Tips

Every state has its own laws for what can and can't be included in a formal offer. Make sure your offer conforms to the laws of that state. Consider having it prepared or reviewed by a real estate agent or a real estate attorney.

☆ ☆ **WARNING** ☆ ☆

An offer becomes accepted and legally binding only when both parties have signed it. In many situations, the buyer can withdraw an offer unless the seller has already accepted it in writing. Before withdrawing your offer, however, consult with a real estate attorney to make sure you're adhering to local laws. This will also help to ensure you get your deposit returned.

Start by Evaluating the Seller's Asking Price

The *asking price* is the price that the seller is advertising. Consider this figure to be the starting point for a negotiation. Many sellers will set an asking price significantly higher than what they actually expect, leaving plenty of room to negotiate. In some situations, the seller might set the price low in hopes of a quick sale. If this is the case, find out the reason(s). Just because an asking price is advertised in real estate listings, for example, does not mean that the seller is obligated to accept an offer at that price, especially if there is more than one potential buyer bidding on the property.

As you evaluate the asking price, determine if it's reasonable for the condition of the home and current market conditions. Next, think about what you can afford and whether or not the home will require an additional investment for repairs or renovations, either before you move in or within a short time afterwards. Consider the price of similar homes in the community that have sold recently (within the past month or two). Doing this comparison is referred to as reviewing *comps* in the real estate business. ("Comp" is short for *comparative market analysis*, usually a list of recent home sales in the vicinity prepared by a real estate agent to serve as a basis for comparing prices.)

A "similar home" is one that is about the basic age, size, and type close to the home you're interested in. Remember: current market conditions change quickly, so get the most current and accurate data you can find to determine if an asking price is reasonable.

Dream Home Tips

For under $15, you can purchase a detailed comp report for virtually any community or geographic area from the SmartHomeBuy.com web site (www.smarthomebuy.com). The information provided in this detailed report (the site shows a sample), in conjunction with information found in the home's appraisal and in information provided by your agent, should provide valuable insight into how much negotiation will be necessary and how much you should offer initially.

In addition to evaluating the asking price, try to determine the seller's needs as well. Does he or she need to sell the home quickly? If you've been preapproved for a mortgage and have your financing ready to go, will this give you an advantage over other potential buyers? Can you accommodate the seller's desired schedule for the closing and move-in date?

Get the Home Appraised *and* Inspected Early On

An *appraisal* and an *inspection* are two different but equally important things that will provide you with information you need about the home.

An appraisal is done by an independent, licensed home appraiser to provide a timely and reliable estimate of what the home is worth—its current value, based on several criteria, including current market conditions. Mortgage lenders/brokers will require an appraisal of the property you plan to purchase. This is an expense you'll need to cover.

An inspection is done by a licensed home inspector who

Dream Home Tips

An appraisal should include examination of the home's title to ensure that the seller owns the property free and clear and that there are no outside claims (such as liens or encumbrances) on the property. The seller should be willing to pay for an *owner's title policy*, which is insurance against problems with the title.

tours the home, examines it carefully, and evaluates its condition. A home inspector can determine, for example, if and when any major repairs are needed. The inspector is typically hired by the prospective buyer, at his or her expense.

Why do you need an inspection? Because you don't want to discover, several months after purchasing your home, that the roof needs to be repaired, the central air conditioning system needs to be replaced, or the basement leaks seriously every time it rains due to problems with the foundation. These repairs could cost tens of thousands of dollars.

By having the home inspected prior to purchasing it, you can learn of any potential problems and then negotiate with the seller either to make the necessary repairs before the closing (at his or her expense) or to reduce the asking price to enable you to invest the difference later into making the necessary repairs.

A good home inspector is objective, experienced, and knowledgeable. This person will evaluate every aspect of the home, from top to bottom, checking the roof, heating, air conditioning, plumbing, wiring, attic, basement, ceilings, floors, windows, doors, foundation, and even the condition of the major appliances. This type of thorough inspection is particularly critical for older homes.

Your real estate agent should be able to recommend an appraiser and an inspector. You can also find them in the Yellow Pages. The American Society of Home Inspectors web site (www.ashi.org) also offers a free referral service. The National Association of Real Estate Appraisers (www.iami.org/NAREA) allows a search of its membership directory by state and the Appraisal Institute (www.appraisalinstitute.org) allows a search of its membership directory by city and state.

Dream Home Tips

Depending on the location and the size of the home, a basic appraisal should cost between $250 and $350 for a single-family home. A separate home inspection could cost an additional $350 (or more), but could save you thousands. If the home fails the inspection or the inspector uncovers serious problems, you want to retain the right to withdraw your offer and/or have the option of renegotiating with the seller.

Here are some of the things to look for when hiring a home inspector:

- A comprehensive list of everything the inspector will inspect
- A sample report showing the inspector's work
- Insurance to cover any errors or omissions in an inspection
- Experience
- Fee

> ☆ ☆ **WARNING** ☆ ☆
>
> Especially if there's a potential problem with the home, the seller may try to convince you that a home inspection is not necessary. The seller may even state that he or she has several other buyers interested in the property who are not requiring an inspection and that he or she would be more inclined to negotiate with them. Insist on an independent inspection (at your expense) prior to purchasing the home. This will help you learn as much as possible about the home and help you make a more intelligent decision. Knowing about anything that's wrong with the home in advance also puts you in a much stronger negotiating position.

- Qualifications and licensing
- Association memberships (check on their standing in each association)
- References from past clients
- Scheduling (make sure the inspection can fit the buyer's and seller's schedules)

Advice from a Professional Home Inspector

Getting the home properly inspected *before* purchasing it is optional and an additional expense. However, it's highly recommended because it can ultimately save you a fortune.

Joseph Corsetto is the president of the American Society of Home Inspectors (ASHI). He has more than 20 years' experience as a home inspector. In this interview, he offers valuable advice to first-time home buyers on hiring a qualified home inspector and then using the information resulting from the inspection.

According to Corsetto, aside from obtaining a referral from a real estate attorney, a real estate agent, or someone you know and respect, the organization's web site is the best way to find the right home inspector who can meet your needs. If you're about to spend $100,000, $200,000, $500,000, or more on a home, don't you want to make sure you're getting your money's worth and that the home doesn't have any significant problems that will be costly to fix once you take ownership of it?

Dream Home Tips

The American Society of Home Inspectors web site offers a free, online referral service (www.ashi.org) to help home buyers find and hire a qualified and experienced home inspector who is a member of the society.

What is a home inspector and why should a home buyer hire one?

Joseph Corsetto: "A home inspector is someone who evaluates the major system components of the building and evaluates the building's overall condition. This includes everything from the foundation and roof to the bathrooms, kitchen, and general structural components of the building. A home buyer relies on the inspector's experience to identify conditions a buyer might not be familiar with, but that impact the habitability of the home. A buyer wants to know the condition of the major system components in a home, because those are the most expensive things to repair or replace. A buyer wants to know if a building is sound or if there is evidence of significant structural concerns that could equate with expensive structural repairs. Buyers need to know if the building is habitable."

Does a home inspector need to be licensed?

Joseph Corsetto: "There are 30 states in the country that require a home inspector to be licensed. The home buyer's best assurance that they are hire the most qualified individual is for them to hire an ASHI member. We are an association that requires its members to meet extremely stringent membership requirements. Our members need to have more experience than many licensed individuals. The states that don't require a license sometimes have a trade practice or registration act, which means that almost anyone with minimal qualifications can pay a fee to become a registered, certified, or licensed inspector. This doesn't provide any guarantee for the home buyer, however, that the inspector is qualified, capable, or experienced. Hiring an ASHI member ensures you're hiring someone with the proper qualifications, who has passed exams, and who adheres to strict ethics guidelines that eliminate conflict of interest. ASHI requires inspectors to complete at least 250 inspections before they can become a full-fledged member. Our guidelines are more stringent than what's required by the states that require inspectors to be licensed. Our web site offers free referrals for ASHI members throughout the country. A home buyer can find someone based on their ZIP code, to find someone in their area."

When is the best time to begin finding and ultimately hire a home inspector?

Joseph Corsetto: "As soon as contract negotiations between the buyer and seller get under way is the best time to start interviewing and then hiring an inspector. During the interview, find out exactly what services are provided and what the costs for those services are. A lot of times, an inspector will provide additional services, such as termite inspections and radon gas sampling. Depending on where the property is located and its size, the cost of a detailed and thorough inspection starts at $350, but can go up to $800."

What are some of the services a home buyer should expect from the inspector?

Joseph Corsetto: "You want to make sure the inspector is going to do a complete home inspection that adheres to the ASHI standards and guidelines. The goal of the inspection is to protect the interests of the buyer. Upon completion of the inspection, the buyer should receive a detailed, written, narrative inspection report, not just a checklist. A narrative report will provide a lot more information that the buyer can use to determine the true condition of the building. The report should include information about the condition of all of the major system components of the building. The focus of the report should be on things like the roof, structure, electrical, plumbing, foundation, and framing, for example. Smaller items, like peeling paint or wallpaper or worn carpeting, might be listed on the report, but these items aren't too significant."

What happens if a home buyer receives a report that lists serious problems with the home? What should he or she do next?

Joseph Corsetto: "The buyer should review the report carefully and determine what items bother them the most, based on significance and cost. If a problem exists, I recommend sitting down with your attorney to discuss how the items on the report should best be handled. To deal with problems, the buyer has three main options. The buyer can negotiate the repair with the seller, take responsibility to handle the repair themselves at their own expense, or simply walk away from the property and seek out something in better condition. I recommend talking to the seller to see if they're willing to discuss what the repair could entail, what the cost is, and who will be responsible for it. When you buy something at a store, you can take it off the shelf to look at it. If you don't like what you're looking at, you can put it back on the shelf and walk away without making a purchase. Hiring an inspector allows you to take a careful look at what you're buying, before you're committed to buying it. The report you're provided with gives the home buyer the chance to evaluate the true condition of what you're buying."

If the inspector finds a problem, is he or she ever the person who will be hired to repair the problem or provide referrals for someone else who can do the repairs?

Joseph Corsetto: "That would be a conflict of interest. The home inspector should be totally unbiased and have nothing to gain. The inspection should never be a vehicle to generate additional work by the inspector."

When hiring an inspector, what qualifications should the buyer look for?

Joseph Corsetto: "I recommend interviewing the inspector to learn about their training, qualifications, experience, what licenses he or she possesses, and what associations he or she belongs to. One of the biggest misconceptions is that if you pay for a cheap home inspection, you'll receive the same detailed report as you would from someone who costs more money. This is typically not the case. You're paying for someone's experience and qualifications, plus the time it takes them to do a thorough inspection of the home. If you cut corners on cost, you run the risk of not ending up with a truly detailed and complete home inspection."

What's the biggest mistake a home buyer makes when hiring an inspector?

Joseph Corsetto: "Hiring a cheap and unqualified home inspector is one of the biggest mistakes I see first-time home buyers make. Another mistake is that someone will do the research necessary to find a highly qualified inspector, pay for the inspection, but then ignore the information given to them in the inspector's report. This report should be read carefully. A homebuyer should act on any negative information in the report before making their purchase. Make sure you truly understand the condition of the building. After receiving the report from the inspector, it is up to the buyer, and only the buyer, to utilize the information provided and act on it. If there are problematic items listed in the report, resolve them before the closing. A home inspection that is paid for by the buyer becomes the proprietary information owned by the person who paid for it. It is the inspector's obligation to keep the contents of the report confidential and not share their findings with the seller."

Negotiating Your Best Price

Depending on the circumstances, if the seller rejects the initial offer, this stage of the home-buying process can become a negotiation. At all times, this negotiation should be handled in a professional manner. Don't allow your emotions to block your judgment or your communications with the seller (which should ultimately be in writing). Once again, your agent will be able to guide you through this process and hopefully expedite it.

Dream Home Tips

It's always best to avoid getting involved in a bidding war on a property, unless you determine that you absolutely want and need this home and only this home. If this is the case, decide how much over the asking price you're willing to spend and able to afford—and then stick to that limit. During the bidding war, make sure the seller knows your personal situation, especially if it makes you a more attractive bidder. For example, being preapproved for a mortgage is attractive to sellers anxious to sell their property quickly.

Negotiating to buy a home is very much like any other type of business negotiation. You and the seller each have an objective, but to complete the transaction, you establish a meeting of the minds and agreement on all terms of the sale. One of the best ways to kick off a negotiation is to make a fair offer on the property, based on current market conditions. It's OK if your offer is lower than the asking price, as long as you can justify your offer based, for example, on the prices of similar homes recently sold in the area.

Throughout the negotiation process, pay attention to and respect the seller's needs and priorities. Understanding what aspects of the negotiation are particularly important to the seller will help you address his or her concerns. As you do this, "think outside the box." If, for example, the seller absolutely won't budge on the selling price, what will he or she offer that has monetary value? To pay for more of the fees due at closing? To include more of the furniture or fixtures? To pay for additional repairs?

For a negotiation to work, don't expect to get everything you're negotiating for. If you handle your side of the negotiation correctly, you will still probably get many of the things you're asking for, but you will probably have to make compromises. For this reason, it's best to start by negotiating the major areas of concern—such as the selling price and any repairs necessary—and then deal with the smaller issues, points that matter less to both sides and that won't become deal breakers. You should also be willing to walk away from a deal.

These are some of the expenses you can negotiate to get the seller to pay for or at least split with you:

- Buyer's agent fees
- Buyer's closing points
- Home repairs
- Termite inspection
- Home inspection
- Survey/appraisal

Dream Home Tips

One excellent negotiation strategy for deciding who will pay which expenses is to agree to split certain costs down the middle. Again, be willing to make compromises, but negotiate hard to get the major things you want or need.

The negotiation does not have to take place directly between you and the seller. If both of you are represented by agents, those two agents can handle much of the negotiation, with each agent taking direction from the party he or she represents. A real estate agent will have experience negotiating the best deals and know what to expect from this process.

When handling your negotiation, especially if you're not working with an agent, you can discuss issues in person or over the telephone with the seller, but you ultimately want everything put into writing. Be sure to follow up every phone discussion with a detailed letter, fax, or e-mail outlining what was discussed. Oral agreements are not binding.

You'll be in the best possible position going into the negotiation if you can pay in cash, you've already been preapproved for a mortgage, and you do not have a home that must sell before you can buy the home on which you've made the offer. You'll also be at an advantage if the home you're hoping to buy has been vacant for a long time. Every month the home is vacant and unsold represents a significant cost to the seller. The seller may be in more of a hurry to sell (and more flexible with the selling price) if he or she is going through a divorce or is trying to settle an estate, for example.

Dream Home Tips

Making a cash deposit in conjunction (which will typically be held by the seller's agent) shows you're more serious about your offer. If you purchase the home, your deposit will become part of your down payment.

You've Agreed on a Price—Now What?

Agreeing with the seller on a purchase price is a major step toward home ownership, especially if you're already preapproved for your mortgage. The next step is to complete a purchase and sales agreement. That's the topic covered in Chapter 6.

CHAPTER 6

The Purchase and Sale Agreement

WHAT'S IN THIS CHAPTER

- What is a purchase and sale (P&S) agreement?
- What information is incorporated into this document
- Insurance issues

Your quest for home ownership is almost complete! One of the final steps before your closing is developing and signing the *purchase and sale agreement*. And this step is very important.

Dream Home Vocabulary

Purchase and sale agreement—This is a written, legally binding contract that both the buyer and the seller sign and date. It outlines the terms, conditions, contingencies, and timetable for the sale of a property will be sold. It also describes the rights of the buyer and the seller. It's probably the most important document you'll sign in purchasing your home. (Yes, it's very important!)

What Is a Purchase and Sale Agreement?

This document can go by various names, such as *purchase agreement*, *P&S*, *earnest money agreement*, or *purchase contract*. It is a written contract that both the buyer and the seller must sign. It outlines the terms, conditions, contingencies, and timetable for the sale of a property. What should be included in this document varies according to the state and the situation between buyer and seller.

A buyer or a seller can purchase a state-specific P&S from a variety of sources, such as the USlegalforms.com (www.uslegalforms.com/contract-for-sale-real-estate.htm) or Urgent Business Forms.com (www.urgentbusinessforms.com/purchase_agreement.asp) web sites and simply fill in the appropriate blanks. However, it's much better to have this document created or customized by your real estate agent, your lender, or your real estate attorney. No matter who creates it, your real estate attorney should review the P&S carefully before you sign it.

> ☆ ☆ **WARNING** ☆ ☆
>
> Once the buyer and the seller sign this document, they must adhere to it. A buyer who fails to abide by its terms could lose his or her deposit and be liable for damages. Likewise, a seller who fails to meet his or her obligations may also be liable for damages.

The P&S Gets Packed with Important Information

A P&S will be a lengthy document containing a lot of information pertaining to the purchase and sale of the home. Here's a quick rundown of what typically gets included in this extremely important document. The preparer can choose to include additional details and topics. The items of information are listed here alphabetically; the order in which these items appear in the document will vary:

- Amount of the buyer's deposit
- Attorneys' fees
- Buyer's responsibilities
- Buyer's right to inspect the property
- Closing (settlement) costs

- Closing (settlement) date
- Condition of the property
- Deed and title information
- Default terms
- Description of permanently attached fixtures
- Description of the property
- Easements
- Environmental inspection details
- Financing/mortgage information, including the application and commitment letter from the lender
- Inclusions and exclusions (what's included with the sale and what's not)
- IRS filing details
- Lead paint disclosure information
- Liens
- Loan lender fees and charges
- Parties involves (buyer and seller)
- Property insurance and risk of loss policy information
- Radon gas disclosure
- Seller's responsibilities
- Severability details
- Termite inspection details
- Transfer and recording charges
- Zoning ordinances

Dream Home Tips

There is no such thing as a standard purchase and sale agreement. This document will be different for every sale, based on the unique situation and agreement between the buyer and seller. If you choose to use a standard agreement, it's important to have it properly customized with guidance from your real estate agent and/or your attorney.

Dream Home Tips

In addition to a P&S, in most states the seller must also provide a *seller's disclosure statement.* This is a form describing the general condition of the property that's being sold. In this document the seller must disclose to the buyer any known pre-existing problems with the home or property.

The P&S will list anything and everything that's included with the property (as well as items that the seller is excluding), including such things as the carpeting, appliances, attached lighting fixtures, air conditioning unit, and ceiling fans. As a general rule, unless an item is listed as included in the sale, it's not part of the sale.

If the buyer will be obtaining a mortgage to purchase the property, details about the financing terms should be included in the P&S. This document often gives the buyer a specified number of days to obtain financing once the document is signed. From the buyer's standpoint, it should also contain a clause stipulating what happens if, for whatever reason, the buyer can't obtain the necessary financing. (This is commonly referred to as a *sale subject to a mortgage* clause.)

Also from the buyer's standpoint, a *rights to terminate* clause is extremely important. This gives the buyer the option to pull out of the agreement if certain conditions are not met.

Included within this clause should be contingencies if case the property fails an inspection or environmental hazards are discovered, for example.

If the P&S has not been created by someone representing you, make sure it does not contain a clause by which you waive your various rights. Some developers try to hide this type of clause within their contracts. If included, such a clause could dramatically limit your rights and the protection otherwise provided to the buyer under the law.

It goes without saying (but it's being said anyway) that you should never sign any legal document that you don't fully understand. Take the time to review the P&S and all related documents with your agent and/or attorney prior to signing them. Once you sign a contract or other legal document, it becomes binding regardless of whether or not you fully understood its contents and ramifications.

Protect Your Investment with Insurance

Prior to the closing, you'll need to acquire several types of insurance, which should immediately go into effect after the closing, when you take on ownership of the home. It's important to possess different types of home-related insurance for protection against a wide range of potential catastrophes and problems. The cost of these insurance policies will depend on the value of what's being covered and the deductibles you set (if applicable).

Just as you would for any other product or service, you'll want to invest some time in determining your needs, shopping around for the best insurance deals, and making sure that the coverage you're purchasing is adequate. Start by sitting down with several insurance agents or brokers. Many real estate agents can also sell home insurance. If you need a referral for an insurance agent or broker, check with someone you know, search online, or check the Yellow Pages.

To learn more about homeowner's insurance, what it covers, what it doesn't cover, and the types of policies available, visit the Insurance Information Institute web site at www.iii.org.

> **Dream Home Tips**
>
> **Make sure you sit down** with your insurance agent or broker to carefully access your needs. Being under-insured can result in financial loss in the event of a catastrophe.

These are some types of insurance you'll most likely need when purchasing your home:

- **Title insurance**—This is purchased at the time of the closing for a one-time fee. It protects you in the event that the property's title is found to be invalid or to have some other problem. Depending on the type of policy, title insurance can protect lenders (up to the mortgage value of the property) or owners (the purchase price of the property).
- **Homeowner's insurance**—This insurance protects your property against fire and theft, for example, and provides necessary liability coverage. This insurance covers

both your home and the contents, including your furniture, valuables, clothing, and other belongings. Most policies require a separate insurance rider for high-priced items, like expensive jewelry, collectibles, or artwork. Your homeowner's insurance should also cover your living expenses in the event of a disaster that makes your home temporarily uninhabitable. The cost of this insurance will vary, based on the value of the property and your belongings, the coverage limit, and the size of your deductible. For further protection, make sure your homeowner's insurance policy takes effect the day prior to your move so that its protects your possessions during your move. Liability protection is necessary in case someone gets injured within your home or on your property. It protects you and other members of your household, including your pets, against liability for causing accidental bodily injury or property damage.

- **Flood insurance**—This type of insurance is typically required if your home is in a region designated as a high-flood-risk area. Flood insurance is issued by the federal government and will cover both your home and its contents, up to a specified amount. For more information, check the National Flood Insurance Program web site, at www.floodsmart.gov.
- **Home warranties**—This is insurance typically for new homes. It ensures that necessary work or repairs will be completed once the owner takes possession of a newly

constructed home, especially if the builder refuses to do the work. This insurance generally covers workmanship for one year, mechanical problems for up to two years, and structural defects in the home for up to ten years. A home warranty can also be issued for an existing home, but its coverage will be more limited.

- **Other insurance**—Separate policies can be purchased to cover everything from earthquakes, hurricanes, and tornados to extremely expensive jewelry, artwork, or collectibles.

☆ ☆ WARNING ☆ ☆

If you'll be obtaining a mortgage, the lender will require you to maintain a specified level of insurance on your home. If you allow the policy to lapse by not paying the premiums, for example, the lender could foreclose on your mortgage. If a disaster happens, you could also find yourself without any insurance protection. Make sure the insurance you purchase covers you and your equity in the property, as well as your lender's interests, and then make sure you stay up-to-date on your premiums.

☆ ☆ ☆

All insurance policies have exclusions and coverage limits. It's important to obtain adequate coverage to meet your needs. It's easy to save money by lowering your insurance coverage and/or raising your deductibles. However, if disaster strikes, you'll want to be covered.

When you begin discussing insurance coverage needs with your insurance agent or broker, you'll be able to choose between coverage that offers different levels of coverage and compensates you in different ways. *Actual cash value* coverage reimburses only for the current cash value of what was lost, *not* the replacement cost. Thus, if you bought a large screen TV for $4,000, it might be worth only $2,500 now. If something happened to it, your insurance would reimburse you the actual cash value; you'd receive only $2,500 (minus any deductibles).

Replacement cost coverage reimburses fully for repair or replacement, with no consideration of depreciation. This is the better coverage to have, but it also costs more. *Guaranteed or extended replacement cost* coverage is the highest level of protection. Even if the cost to replace or repair whatever is lost exceeds the policy limit, it will be fully covered. This covers your loss if the cost to repair or replace is higher than what you paid for it.

It is essential to choose the right type of insurance, set adequate coverage limits, and set appropriate deductibles. However, overinsuring or buying overlapping policies can be a waste of money. A reputable and knowledgeable insurance broker or agent will be able to evaluate your needs and make recommendations based on your personal and financial situation.

It's important to have adequate insurance coverage. It's equally important to choose an insurance company that's highly rated, well established, and respected in the industry. To determine if an insurance company is well-rated, contact one or more of the following:

- Standard and Poor's (212 208-1199, www2.standardand-poors.com)
- Moody's Investors Services (800 811-6980, www.moodys.com)
- Weiss Ratings Inc. (800 289-9222, www.weissratings.com)
- Duff & Phelps, LLC (312 368-3198, www.duffand-phelps.com)

Consumer Reports magazine (www.consumerreports.org) also rates homeowner's insurance companies.

Understand and keep in mind the difference between an insurance *agent* and an insurance *broker*. An agent might represent only one insurance company, while a broker will most likely represent several insurance companies and work on a commission.

Dream Home Tips

One way to protect your possessions is to maintain a detailed inventory of everything you own. In addition to keeping a written list (in a safe place, such as a bank safe deposit box or fireproof safe in your home), is also very smart to keep a video or photographic record of your things. If you save receipts for high-priced items and keep a list of relevant serial numbers, model numbers, etc., those records will be extremely important if you ever have to file an insurance claim as a result of theft, fire, or another catastrophe. The Insurance Information Institute "Know Your Stuff" web site (www.knowyourstuff.org) offers a free home inventory software package you can use to document your possessions.

☆ ☆ **WARNING** ☆ ☆

After you pay off your mortgage in full, you will no longer be required to maintain an active homeowner's insurance policy. It'll be entirely up to you to maintain this coverage, but it's highly recommended that you do.inspection (at your expense) prior to purchasing the home. This will help you learn as much as possible about the home and help you make a more intelligent decision. Knowing about anything that's wrong with the home in advance also puts you in a much stronger negotiating position.

It's Time for Your Closing!

Now that you've found your dream home, negotiated an acceptable price with the seller, signed your purchase and sale agreement, and acquired the necessary insurance, you're just about ready for the closing! This is the final step in the home-buying process. Get ready to make everything official.

You're about to make one of the biggest and most significant purchases of your life. While this can be scary, if you've got qualified professionals—real estate agent, mortgage broker/lender, and attorney—the process should go smoothly and be relatively free of hassles. The next chapter focuses on the closing process.

CHAPTER 7

The Closing: Congratulations! You're Almost a Homeowner

WHAT'S IN THIS CHAPTER

- Understanding the closing process
- What to expect at your closing
- What you'll need to bring to your closing
- Avoiding common problems at your closing

The process of buying your home is almost over! Soon, you'll be able to move in and begin your new life as a homeowner. One of the final steps in the process is the *closing* (aka *settlement*). This is when all of the contracts and legal documents get signed and the property changes ownership from the seller to the buyer. Don't worry! Your real estate attorney, your real estate agent, and possibly your mortgage broker will be present during this process to guide you. Be prepared to sign dozens upon dozens of legal documents, forms, and contracts.

The closing may sound like it's the end of something important; however, in reality it's the beginning. Once the closing is over, you will be the proud owner of your home and no longer a renter. Thus, your new homeowner status is potentially the start of something wonderful.

At the closing, all of the parties may be present—you and the people listed above and the seller and his or her attorney and real estate agent. The closing agent (or an attorney) will conduct the meeting. It's that person's job to collect all of the necessary paperwork in advance and make sure that all documents are ready to be signed. When all of the parties attend the closing, it's called a *round table closing*. However, a closing can also take place with each party separately, using an escrow process overseen by the closing agent. This is called an *escrow closing*. All the documents, payments, and any adjustments are delivered to a neutral third party; then, on the scheduled day, the *escrow agent* delivers the deed and money.

You may hear the terms *wet settlement* and *dry settlement*. A *wet settlement* is when the funds are available for the closing and the seller gets them right away. The closing agent is there with a cashier's check or the money is wired into the seller's account at the same time as the parties are closing. A *dry settlement* is when there is no money for the seller at the closing. Usually, the settlement company or attorney will complete the documents and submit them to the lender for review; then the lender will provide the funds.

What Is a Closing?

The closing is one of the final steps in the home-buying process. It takes place when the buyer and the seller have reached an agreement, the necessary financing has been approved, and all of the documents necessary for the transaction have been prepared and are ready to be signed. Prior to the closing, you must obtain a *letter of commitment* from your lender, stating that you have been approved for the mortgage and that the funds to purchase the home will be made available to you at the closing.

Dream Home Vocabulary

> ***Letter of commitment***–A letter from the mortgage broker or lender stating that you've been approved for a mortgage and specifying the amount of the loan and the terms.

At the closing, the terms of the agreement between you and the seller will be reviewed. At the same time, the terms of the agreement between you and your mortgage lender will also be reviewed. When all of the documents have been signed, you will receive your mortgage (the money you're borrowing to purchase the home). You and the seller will execute the sales contract; at this point, ownership of the home transfers from the seller to you. Finally, all of the various fees and expenses associated with the purchase are distributed to the appropriate parties.

Scheduling your closing can be tricky, because it must happen before the *loan commitment* you receive from your lender expires, but you need ample time to ensure that all of the paperwork is completed and that any work on the home has been finished prior to the closing. Your real estate agent or the seller's agent will provide guidance and probably schedule the closing at the appropriate time.

Within 24 hours before the closing, make an appointment to walk through the home and conduct a final inspection. Depending on the situation, your real estate agent should be present. You might also want to bring along a home inspector, if there's any recent construction or major repair work. The purpose of this walk-through is to ensure that there's been no recent damage to the home and that the seller has completed all of the repairs to which he or she has agreed. At this point, the home should be in the condition specified in your purchase and sale agreement.

During the final inspection, make sure that everything is present that was specified in the purchase and sale agreement as included with the house. This might include appliances, window treatments, lighting fixtures, and furniture. If you haven't negotiated for these items to be included in the purchase and they're not listed in the purchase and sale agreement, you're not entitled to them.

Dream Home Tips

Some states require the buyer to have an attorney representing him or her at the closing. Regardless of what your state requires, hiring a competent real estate attorney to be with you at the closing and to review all of the documents before you sign them is an excellent strategy to ensure that all of your legal and financial interests are being met.

You have the right to request copies of all documents 24 hours in advance of the closing, so you and your attorney have ample time to review them. This is an opportunity to ensure that everything you've agreed to is stated properly in the documents that will become legally binding as soon as you sign them at the closing.

Be Prepared at the Closing

At the closing, you'll need to sign dozens of legal documents. It's the closing agent's responsibility to prepare all of the documents in advance. However, mistakes and typos happen, so it's a good idea to review everything.

You are responsible for bringing the following to the closing:

- A copy of your new homeowner's insurance policy and

copies of all related insurance policies, plus proof of payment for those policies, so you can show they're in force.

- A certified check to cover all closing costs and your down payment on the home. The closing agent will tell you the exact amount of that check prior to the closing. Personal checks are rarely accepted. If you plan to wire the funds, coordinate this transaction several days in advance. Of course, cash is always accepted.
- One or two forms of photo identification (driver's license and/or passport) to prove your identity prior to signing any documents.

Dream Home Tips

The money due at the closing will be specified on the HUD-1 Settlement Statement, which the closing agent should provide to you at least 24 hours prior to the closing. The HUD-1 lists all of the services provided and the associated fees that you are responsible for paying. You should be aware of and approve all of these fees in advance. You can see the HUD-1 Settlement Statement here: www.hudclips.org/sub_nonhud/html/pdfforms/1.pdf.

Fees Associated with the Closing

Buying a home isn't cheap. Many people receive fees in order for this process to happen. Here are some of the fees that you'll be responsible for paying at the closing:

- **Appraisal fee**—This fee, typically under $300 for a single-family home or condominium, is to be paid when the appraisal is done or before the work is done. The appraisal helps to determine the current value of the home you're buying and is required by the lending (mortgage) company. The appraisal is conducted by an independent, licensed professional. Your lender will typically choose the appraiser, although you will be responsible for the fee.

- **Application fee**—Depending on the situation, you may be required to pay the application fee for the mortgage when you apply for it. This fee is intended to cover what it costs the lender or mortgage broker to process your application. This fee varies dramatically from company to company and what you pay could, in part, be determined by your credit score and the type of mortgage.
- **Loan origination fee**—The lender or mortgage broker charges this fee to offset the institution's costs and earn a profit. This fee can be a percentage of the loan amount. Loan origination fees vary greatly, so it's important to shop around for the best deals and negotiate.
- **Discount points**—You pay this fee at the closing to lower the interest rate on your loan. Basically, it allows you to prepay finance charges in order to save money over the life of the loan.
- **Taxes**—These are fees charged by local governments to transfer ownership of the property. The taxes collected at the closing could also represent prorated annual real estate

(property) taxes that are due. The taxes will vary greatly, depending on where the home is located. These fees cannot be negotiated down. However, you may be able to split them with the seller, if you negotiate this in advance.

- **Miscellaneous fees**—Depending on your situation, you may be required to pay other fees at the closing, which will be outlined in advance. For example, if you're taking over the seller's mortgage, you may be required to pay a transfer or assumption fee. If you're purchasing a condominium, you may be required to pay condominium fees at the closing.

Dream Home Vocabulary

Closing Costs—These are all fees, charges, and taxes you'll be required to pay at the closing. Each fee, charge, and tax will be itemized on the HUD-1 statement and can include payment required for points, taxes, title insurance, and financing costs.

Some of the other charges for which you may be responsible (which will be specified on the HUD-1) are administrative fees, credit report retrieval fees, underwriting fees, title examination fees, title insurance fees, document preparation fees, escrow fees, pest inspection fees, recording fees, and survey fees. In addition to the fees associated with the mortgage, you may also have to pay fees to your real estate agent. Depending on the situation, it's not uncommon for fees due at closing to be $10,000 or more. It is sometimes possible, however, to build some or all of these fees into the loan, so you pay little or nothing out of pocket at the closing.

Dream Home Tips

Some of the fees can be negotiated in advance so you can potentially save money. Certain fees have fixed rates and cannot be adjusted or waived.

Navigating Through Piles and Piles of Paperwork

Despite the fact that computers play a key role in just about everything, when it comes to the closing, virtually all paperwork is done traditionally, on paper. Consequently, hundreds of sheets of paper are generated in the sale of a home or a condo.

Some of the documents associated with a closing are the *HUD-1 Settlement Statement*, the *truth-in-lending statement*, the *mortgage note*, and the *deed of trust*. Your attorney will review each of these documents with you. Take the time to ensure that all of the numbers, terms, and information on these forms and contracts are accurate before signing them. Regardless of any verbal agreements that you reach with the seller or the lender, it's whatever is in black and white within these documents that will be legally binding.

Dream Home Vocabulary

Mortgage note—This is the formal written agreement between the home buyer and the lender. It's a legally binding agreement that includes the buyer's promise to repay the debt. It also details the terms of the loan and specifies penalties that could be imposed if payments are late or missed or if the loan goes into default.

☆ ☆ **WARNING** ☆ ☆

A dishonest mortgage broker or lender may make last-minute changes in the loan terms, such as raising the interest rate. You may never have discussed these changes, but they could appear in the paperwork at the closing. If you sign documents with changes, you are legally accepting those changes because the documents are then legally binding. By working with an attorney who represents you (not the seller), you reduce the chances of this happening.

Dream Home Vocabulary

Deed of trust—If the home buyer fails to meet his or her financial obligations and make the monthly mortgage payments, this document gives the lender legal claim to the home and property. It also includes a summary of the legal rights of both the lender and the borrower, such as the ability of the lender to foreclose on the home if the loan goes into default.

Here are some of the many other documents you may be required to sign at the closing:

- *Name affidavit*—a document listing your full name and all of the aliases you currently use or have used in the past
- *Occupancy affidavit*—a document stating that you intend to live in the home you're purchasing and that it will be your primary residence
- *Payment letter*—a document that specifies your monthly mortgage payment, when it's due, and where you should send it

- *Form 4506*—an IRS form, *Request for Copy of Tax Form*, allowing the lender to obtain and review copies of your tax returns and other tax-related documents to verify your income

Shortly after your closing (or perhaps several months later), your loan may be transferred to another lender or investor that will then service it (i.e., collect your monthly mortgage payments). This is a common practice. At the closing, you will be notified if this is a possibility.

Depending on the type of mortgage, your monthly payment will most likely consist of four components—principal, interest, taxes, and insurance. If the down payment on your home is less than 20 percent of the purchase price, you'll most likely need to acquire *private mortgage insurance (PMI)*, which you will pay in advance at the closing or will be added into your monthly mortgage payments. If you have a good credit score, there are several strategies for avoiding the necessity of paying PMI; your broker can advise you.

Although you'll be confronted at the closing with hundreds of papers to review and sign, there's no need to become anxious, especially if you have a real estate attorney sitting next to you reviewing all of the documents and explaining their significance before you sign them. Assuming that all of the parties show up for the closing on time and all of the paperwork is in order, the closing should take under one hour.

Dream Home Tips

Unfortunately, it's common for mistakes to be noticed in the paperwork or for documents to be missing at the closing. Don't panic if this happens. Your attorney will know exactly how to proceed and advice you accordingly. Typically, unless a mistake is significant, the closing will continue on schedule and small corrections to documents will be made later. In some situations, it may be necessary to delay the closing until all of the documents are corrected and ready to be signed.

Closing-Related Mistakes to Avoid

In the days and weeks leading up to your closing, there are some things you should do to avoid unnecessary complications.

For example, refrain from making any major purchases or applying for credit cards. Purchasing a car or other big-ticket items could cause problems with the mortgage broker or lender. If you need to make a major purchase, wait until after the closing to ensure that it won't affect your credit score or somehow jeopardize your ability to get approved for the mortgage.

Also, in the weeks leading up to your closing, don't change jobs. Obviously, this includes not getting laid off or fired. This could negatively impact the approval process for your mortgage. Lenders typically prefer a consistent job history. If you need to change employers, do this after the closing. (Earning a raise or a promotion with your current employer is fine.)

If you'll be paying money to the seller, such as the down payment, make sure this money goes into a trust or escrow account until the closing. You don't want the seller spending your money before the house is officially yours.

In addition to homeowner's insurance and mortgage insurance, consider hazard insurance and make sure your new home is insured adequately. To avoid any complications at the closing, make sure you acquire all of the necessary insurance in advance and that you bring the paperwork to prove that you've paid for the policies and they're in force.

Make sure you schedule a final walk-through of the home the day before the closing. Your real estate agent will help you tie up any loose ends and make sure everything is ready for the closing. During your walk-through, if you notice any problems, make sure you bring them to the attention of the seller and your real estate agent immediately. For example, as the seller was moving out of the home, perhaps damage to a doorway or wall happened. You want to ensure that the seller will take care of repairing the damage prior to the closing. This walk-through should be in addition to a professional inspection, which should be completed by an independent home inspector who will be able to explore the home and identify problems and defects that you might not notice.

Dream Home Tips

Chapter 5 features an in-depth interview with Joseph Corsetto, president of the American Society of Home Inspectors. In this interview, he provides advice for hiring and using the services of a home inspector.

During the home inspection, a licensed home inspector will check for potential problems with the following, in particular:

- Air conditioning and heating system
- Basement and foundation
- Electrical system and wiring
- Interior and exterior framing and overall construction
- Plumbing
- Roof
- Ventilation and insulation

Dream Home Tips

Just prior to the closing, your lender will supply you with a list of documents you'll need to bring to the closing. To avoid delays, remember to bring everything that's expected.

☆ ☆ WARNING ☆ ☆

The listing agent or the real estate agent who represents the seller does not represent you, the buyer! This person will *not* be working in your best interest, financially or otherwise. No matter how professional and pleasant the agent is to you, never assume he or she is offering you the best price or giving you all of the information you need to make a well-informed purchase decision. Unless you hired the attorney to represent you, he or she can not provide you with legal advice and is in no way obligated to look out for your best interests.

Another common mistake among first-time home buyers is making verbal agreements with the seller and/or the lender. Everything you agree to should ultimately be documented in writing and then both parties should sign and date the documents. This ensures a mutual and legally binding understanding of the agreement.

Perhaps the biggest mistake home buyers make is taking on too much debt. Before the closing, review all of the numbers and your budget. Make sure you can afford to purchase the home and will be able to stay current on your mortgage payments, properly maintain the home, and afford all of the costs associated with owning a home, such as insurance and real estate taxes. Hopefully, you've done all of your financial calculations and budgeting much earlier in the process. Just because you've been approved for a large mortgage to cover the cost of the home doesn't necessarily mean you can afford it. It's up to you to make this determination—not the lender or mortgage broker.

Depending on the type of mortgage you're acquiring, make sure that if real estate prices in your area drop for some reason, but you haven't built up a lot of equity in your new home, you won't wind up owing more money than the home is worth. You could always hang onto the home in hopes real estate values will rise again, but if you need to sell at some point in order to relocate for a job, you could run into costly problems if you're overextended financially.

Congratulations, You Are a Homeowner!

Upon completion of the closing, you'll officially be a homeowner! The deed for the property and the house keys will be in your hands. You are now responsible for making your monthly mortgage payments on time for the term of the mortgage.

Once the closing has ended, you'll be given copies of the documents you've signed. Keep all of these papers together in a safe place. You'll need to refer back to them in the future if and when you decide to refinance your mortgage or sell the home.

With the closing behind you, it's time to plan your move into your new home, decorate your home, unpack your stuff, and start your new life in your new neighborhood. Chapter 8 focuses on packing and moving.

Dream Home Tips

Chances are, by the time the closing is completed, you'll be happy to complete the process. Down the road, however, it might make sense for you to refinance your mortgage to obtain a lower interest rate, for example. If your credit score improves or interest rates drop, refinancing could save you thousands, so keep your options open. When acquiring a mortgage, negotiate the terms so you'll have no prepayment penalties if you later decide to pay it off early or refinance it.

CHAPTER 8

Planning Your Move

WHAT'S IN THIS CHAPTER

- Notifying your landlord that you'll be moving out
- Packing up your stuff
- Hiring a mover
- Contacting the utility companies
- Filing a change of address with the U.S. Postal Service

You've probably discovered by now that finding, buying, and moving into your new home is a time-consuming and life-altering process. The next phase of the process involves packing up your stuff and moving out of your current home and into your new home. This chapter will help you prepare to move out and tie up loose ends.

You need to start preparing for your move at least two to three months before moving day. This will give you ample time to properly handle all of the necessary details and ensure a well-organized and cost-effective move. Of course, you can speed up this process, but you'll probably run into additional costs, such as having to pay for at least one or two extra months of rent in order to break your lease.

These are the basic steps involved in preparing for a move:

- Contact your landlord to discuss breaking your lease, if you have one. If you're renting from month to month, if your lease has expired, or if you didn't sign a lease, skip this step.
- Pack up your possessions.
- Hire a mover or rent a moving truck.
- Contact your current and future utility companies.
- File a change of address with the U.S. Postal Service, companies you do business with, and your personal acquaintances.

Contacting Your Current Landlord

If you're moving from an apartment where your lease hasn't yet expired, if you plan to break the lease and want to avoid potentially high legal fees and other charges, it's important to contact your landlord and negotiate a fair settlement that will allow you to move out before your lease expires.

With 45 to 60 days' notice, most landlords can find a new tenant for the apartment and will not penalize the current tenant financially. Some landlords, however, are less willing to work with tenants who want or need to break their lease. If you're in that situation, you'll probably have to negotiate with the landlord to reach a financial settlement that's mutually acceptable. This might mean allowing the landlord to keep your deposit or paying one or two months' rent after you move out. If several months remain before the lease expires, a landlord is unlikely to force you to pay the entire amount owed, as long as you provide ample notice before you move.

If you're renting an apartment from month to month, your landlord will probably require you to provide at least 30 days' notice before moving or you could be held responsible for paying an extra month's rent.

☆ ☆ **WARNING** ☆ ☆

Simply moving out in the middle of the night when you still have several months left on your lease does not relieve you of your legal and financial responsibilities to the landlord.

Dream Home Tips **If you have problems negotiating** with your landlord, contact a lawyer who can advise you of your legal rights, based on where you live and the situation you're in.

Ten Tips for Packing up Your Stuff

As you get ready to leave your current residence and move into your new home, you'll need to either pack up all of your belongings yourself or hire a full-service mover that includes a packing. Packing can be a tedious and time-consuming job. It's important, however, to take a well-organized approach, so you'll be able to unpack in your new home with relative ease.

Here are ten packing tips:

1. Pack one room at a time. Label each box with a description of its contents and its destination (e.g., kitchen, bedroom closet, bathroom, etc.). Being as specific as possible in your descriptions will make unpacking faster and easier. Plus, you'll be able to find items you need quickly.
2. When packing a car or truck, make sure you load in last the items or boxes you'll need first once you reach your new home. For many people, that includes cleaning supplies.
3. Pack all boxes to their capacity. If a box isn't totally filled, it is more likely to get crushed. However, don't fill your boxes to the point where they could tear or break.
4. Keep the weight of your boxes reasonable, based on your strength and ability to carry, stack, and move them. If possible, put heavy items in small boxes to make them easier

to carry. When carrying any heavy items, wear a back brace and/or use a dolly.

5. Double-box fragile items and be sure to add plenty of cushioning, such as crumpled paper or polystyrene foam or biodegradable packing peanuts.
6. As a general rule, to reduce your packing, don't pack stuff you don't want or need. If you won't need something in your new home, donate it to charity, sell it at a garage sale, or auction it on eBay (www.ebay.com) *before* you move.
7. Use Space Bag storage packs (800 617-4190, www.space-bag.com) for pillows, blankets, towels, linens, and bulky clothes. These transparent bags shrink when you use your vacuum cleaner to suck out the air. These bags will also protect your belongings from mold, mildew, and dirt. You can purchase an assortment of storage packs for under $20.
8. To avoid losing or accidentally throwing out small items, wrap fragile knickknacks and other items in brightly colored tissue paper before putting them into boxes.
9. Use only unprinted newsprint paper to wrap items. The ink from regular newspapers will transfer to your belongings and could ruin them.
10. Don't reuse boxes that have been used many times or that are showing signs of wear. Each box should be sturdy enough to hold what you put inside it and be strong enough to be placed on the bottom of a stack without crushing, tearing, or falling apart.

Hiring a Mover or Renting a Moving Truck

Once you know where you're going to move and you've set your moving date, it's time to figure out how you'll transport your belongings from your old residence to your new home. You have three primary options:

- Hiring a full-service mover
- Hiring a pickup-and-delivery service or self-service mover
- Planning a do-it-yourself move

Dream Home Tips

Moving.com and moving.move.com are two of many online resources for helping plan moves. Many real estate agents, moving supply companies, and moving companies offer similar resources.

Full-Service Movers

Hiring a full-service mover is the most costly option, but it also means the fewest hassles for you. A full-service mover will provide all packing materials, help you pack your stuff, load the moving truck, drive the truck to your new home, and unload your belongings. In other words, these services handle just about every aspect of your physical move.

There are numerous factors that go into calculating the cost of a full-service mover. When comparing price quotes from movers, make sure that each quote is for the services you want and need. Here are some of the factors:

- The number of laborers (movers) required

- The size of the truck
- The time of year (and even the time of the month)
- The distance of the move
- The amount of belongings you'll be moving
- The time that the moving company anticipates the move will take (in labor hours)

Shop around for the best price before hiring a full-service mover. If possible, hire a company based on a referral, so you know the company is reliable. Obviously, your goal should be to hire a professional mover that is experienced and insured, has an excellent reputation, and comes highly recommended by a friend or relative.

Before hiring a mover, you can contact the Better Business Bureau (www.bbb.org) and Chamber of Commerce in your area to make sure the company you're considering is reputable. The full-service mover you hire should be registered and/or licensed by the state's Department of Transportation. One way to determine if a moving company is legitimate is to contact the Department of Transportation in your state.

As you shop around for a mover and obtain price quotes from companies, you'll always be asked a series of questions. The moving companies will want to know your current location and your destination, in order to calculate the number of miles between locations. (The cost of your move will be based, in part, on the distance.)

You'll also be asked to describe how much stuff is to be packed and moved. Be prepared to answer questions like these:

- How many fully furnished rooms are in your current home?
- How full are the rooms?
- What types of appliances and large pieces of furniture are being moved?

Based on the information you provide, moving companies will attempt to calculate the weight of your belongings and the number of people necessary to pack your things, load the truck, make the move, and unload the truck. The companies will then provide you with a free written quote or estimate that falls into one of these three categories:

- **Binding Quote.** This is a guaranteed price, within a small percentage of deviation. This price is based on a complete list of items to be moved and the services to be performed. To provide a binding quote, a representative from the moving company will inspect your current residence and belongings.
- **Nonbinding or Hourly Rate Quote.** This quote will be little more than a detailed list of what the moving company charges for each of its services. The rates should, however, be based on the movers' experience with jobs similar to yours. Until the move is completed, you won't be able to calculate the exact cost. The company will recommend the number of movers, the size of the truck, and the types of supplies needed; roughly estimate how long the job will take and the cost based on a per-hour fee; and add costs for supplies, mileage, and other charges.

- **Not-to-Exceed Quote.** The cost of the job is guaranteed not to be higher than the quote. For the mover, the quoted price is binding as the maximum. However, if the move costs less than estimated, you'll be charged that lower amount.

Dream Home Tips

As you collect estimates or price quotes from movers, make sure that all agreements and details are in writing and signed and dated by all parties. If you obtain more than one estimate and the ranges vary greatly, ask enough questions to determine the reasons for the differences.

Prior to the move, the people hired to pack, load, and unload should come to your current residence and review every item to be transported. The movers should check for any damage. Be present for this inspection and look for items that are bent, burned, broken, chipped, dented, gouged, rusted, covered in mildew, scratched, warn, torn, soiled, faded, or loose. The movers will give you a written assessment; make sure you fully agree with it before the items are packed and moved.

Hiring a full-service moving company will make the physical part of your move faster and easier. However, even if you hire a full-service moving company, there are certain things you'll definitely want to pack yourself and transport with you and not in the moving truck. This list should include all of your valuables (including jewelry), memorabilia, family heirlooms, collectibles, firearms, photo albums, items used in conjunction with your hobbies, medications, and anything else that's worth a lot, that can't easily be replaced, or that you want to have accessible before the movers unload the truck.

Dream Home Tips

From the American Moving and Storage Association web site (www.moving.org), you can download a free, 14-page moving guide, *Consumer Handbook: A Practical Guide to Interstate Moving.* It offers information and advice, including factors to consider when hiring a mover.

Pickup-and-Delivery Movers and Self-Service Movers

If you can't afford to hire a full-service mover, but you don't want to drive a truck or deal with the responsibility of a do-it-yourself move, another option is to hire a pickup-and-delivery (PUD) service or self-service moving company.

You don't have to drive the truck, but you are responsible for your own packing, unpacking and manual labor. After evaluating your needs, a mover will help you determine the size of truck you need and then deliver it to your current residence, typically at least two days prior to the actual moving date. It's then your responsibility to pack up all of your belongings and load the truck yourself.

Once the truck is fully loaded, a professional driver picks it up and drives it to your new home. Then you unload and unpack. The price you pay for this service is based primarily on the weight of your load and the distance of your move.

For this type of move, you are responsible for purchasing all moving supplies, such as boxes, packing tape, and any padding.

> ☆ ☆ **WARNING** ☆ ☆
>
> Do not cancel your current renter's insurance before your new homeowner's insurance begins. It's absolutely critical that all of your furniture and possessions are insured during the actual move. Make sure there is no lapse in coverage. If you don't currently have renter's insurance, have your homeowner's insurance coverage begin before you move.

There's another option, an alternative to using a truck—containers. One company that offers this option is Door To Door Storage and Moving, www.doortodoor.com.

The company brings sturdy containers that are 8′ x 5′ x 7′. Each can hold the contents of one to one and a half rooms. You take as long as you want to load the containers and pay only for the containers you use. You lock the containers and call the company.

The company then picks up the containers, securing each with a tamper-proof seal, and ships them by truck. The company tells you exactly when your containers will arrive and how much the move will cost, upfront.

There are disadvantages. One is that the company does not serve all areas of the United States. Another disadvantage is that moves can take longer than with traditional moving companies.

The Do-It-Yourself Move

Doing your move yourself will require pricing out and paying for each part of the moving process separately and then packing, loading, driving, unloading, and unpacking. The benefit to a do-it-yourself move is that you can set your own schedule and save a fortune. The drawback is that you'll need to recruit a few of your friends or relatives to help and you'll need to do the heavy lifting.

In taking the do-it-yourself approach, you'll need to consider the following costs and calculate them into your budget:

- Dolly rental
- Fuel charges (for the truck and/or your vehicle)
- Furniture pads
- Hourly laborers—or refreshments for your volunteers
- Insurance
- Packing materials (boxes, tape, bubble wrap, etc.)
- Tolls
- Truck mileage charges
- Truck rental
- Warehouse/storage fees

By doing it yourself, you have total control over scheduling, but you're also taking sole responsibility for all of your belongings. If you pack something incorrectly and it breaks, it's your own fault.

If you check the Yellow Pages or contact any moving truck rental company, you'll find a wide selection of vehicles you can rent. The size of the vehicle (truck, van, or trailer) you choose should be based upon how much stuff you need to transport, how many trips you plan to make, and cost.

When shopping around for the best deal on a vehicle, you can check the Yellow Pages for local companies or contact one of the following national truck rental companies:

- Budget Truck Rentals: (800) 462-8343, www.budget-truck.com
- Hertz Truck and Van Rental: (888) 999-5500, www.hertztrucks.com
- Penske Truck Rental: (888) 996-5415, www.pensketruck-rental.com
- U-Haul: (800) 468-4285, www.uhaul.com

Dream Home Tips

When you rent a vehicle, you'll pay a flat daily fee plus mileage and insurance. You'll also be responsible for gas, tolls, and other related expenses. Be sure to calculate these expenses into your moving budget. Don't be fooled by a truck rental ad that says, "$19.95 per day rental," for example. There are always additional fees to consider.

In order to decide what size truck you'll need, U-Haul recommends the following:

- To move the contents of an apartment or condo will require a smaller vehicle, such as a 10-foot truck, with 368 cubit feet of space (5′ x 10′ x 8′). You can also rent a van or a sport utility vehicle or, if you have a vehicle, a trailer. If you rent a trailer, you'll need a hitch, which you can rent or buy from the rental dealer.

- To move the contents of two standard-size rooms, a 5′ x 8′ trailer (208 cubic feet of space) is suitable. To move the contents of three standard-size (furnished) rooms, a 6′ x 12′ trailer (396 cubic feet of space) is suitable.
- For larger moves, you can rent trucks. A 26-foot truck has 1,592 cubic feet of space.

Dream Home Tips

No matter what size truck you rent, make sure you can lock up your belongings safely, using your own padlock.

Get plenty of padding, such as blankets for large items and furniture, and rope or straps to secure your possessions. Loads can shift during even short moves. Pack as tightly as possible, from wall to wall and floor to ceiling. For heavy items, it makes sense to use some type of dolly

Before choosing the size of your truck, take a complete inventory of everything you want to move. Measure your larger pieces of furniture. Calculate approximately how many boxes you'll be moving. Once you know your space needs, calculate the distance you'll be moving. Using a web site like Yahoo! Driving Directions (maps.yahoo.com/dd) or MapQuest (www.mapquest.com), you can quickly calculate the exact number of miles between your current address and your new home. When renting a moving truck, you'll need to answer the following questions:

- How long will you need the vehicle (days and hours)?
- What date(s) is the vehicle needed?
- What is the distance (in miles) between your current residence and your new home?
- What size truck is needed? What pieces of furniture and how many boxes are you moving?
- Will you be renting the truck for a one-way move and dropping it off at another location?

Make sure that when you return your rental truck it's fueled up. Many rental companies charge an additional $6 or more per gallon to refill the tank for you.

eMove.com is a free online service that offers local referrals for moving equipment rental, storage, and laborers (to load and unload).

Do you need to move a car or a piano? An auto mover will transport your car from your current residence to your new home, whether it's across the state or across the country. A piano mover has the expertise to transport your instrument safely. For a specialty mover referral, check the Yellow Pages under "Automobile Transport" or "Piano Mover" or visit this web site: www.moving.com/Moving_and_Planning/Quotes/index.asp.

Packing Supplies Checklist

As you begin packing up your furniture and other belongings, it's important to use the right packing materials to ensure that every item will arrive safely and undamaged. The following is a list of moving supplies you'll probably want on hand as you pack, move, and unpack:

- Blankets (to wrap large items and cushion furniture)
- Box labels (including "Fragile" labels)
- Bubble Wrap® or other cushioning material
- Cardboard boxes in various sizes (available from moving companies, truck rental companies, office supply superstores, supermarkets, etc.)
- Dish dividers and boxes
- Dolly (hand truck)
- Markers
- Packing paper (best to avoid using newspapers)
- Packing peanuts
- Packing tape (two inches wide)
- Plastic mattress covers
- Plastic sofa Cover
- Stretch wrap
- Tape gun/dispenser

Dream Home Tips

Companies like U-Haul offer a box buy-back service. Thus, you can purchase a wider assortment and larger quantity of boxes than you expect to need and then return any unused boxes for a full refund. In addition to selling single boxes and boxes in packages of 10, the company also sells box packages. For example, the Box Starter Kit ($99.95) consists of ten 18" x 18" x 16" boxes, 15 16" x 12" x 12" boxes, four rolls of paper tape to seal boxes, one box of Enviro-Bubble® cushioning material, four packages of cushion foam, two box markers, and one utility box knife.

Don't cut corners when packing your personal belongings. Pack each item in the right size of box and use enough packing material to avoid damage. When you purchase your moving supplies, stock up on plenty of boxes of different sizes.

> ☆ ☆ **WARNING** ☆ ☆
>
> When purchasing boxes, think smaller. You're better off packing your stuff in more medium-size boxes rather than fewer large or extra-large boxes. Smaller boxes are easier to carry, stack, and transport. Also, they're better for books and other heavy items. Be sure to use ample padding, such as crumpled paper or packing peanuts.

Contacting Your Utility Companies

Between two and four weeks prior to your move, contact your current utility companies—e.g., electricity, natural gas, local phone, long-distance phone, cable TV, satellite TV, high-speed Internet—to inform them you'll be moving, to terminate service at your current residence on the date of your move, and to arrange to pay your final bill. Depending on where you're moving, you'll then need to contact the utility companies that will be servicing your new address and arrange for service to be turned on. If you're staying within the same service region, you may be able to call each utility and have your services transferred to your new address.

Unfortunately, as you contact each utility, you'll probably have to navigate through a maze of automated voice mail prompts and then sit on hold for a while before speaking with a customer service representative. When contacting each utility, make sure you have a current or recent bill or statement in hand, so you can refer to your customer number and other pertinent information. The phone number to call will also be displayed somewhere on your statement or bill.

Dream Home Tips

MoveUtilities (www.moveutilities.com) is a service that can help you contact your current and future utility companies and transfer service. It allows you to compare providers and order essential home services, including not only utilites but also newspapers, insurance, and banking.

The utilities you'll need to contact probably include the following:

- Electric company
- Gas company
- Cable TV and Internet provider
- Telephone company
- Alarm company

Dream Home Tips

To avoid excess charges when canceling your cable television service, be sure to return your cable box and remote, if applicable, to the cable service provider. This may require a visit to their office.

Filing a Change of Address with the U.S. Postal Service and Others

About 30 days prior to your move, once you know exactly when and where you'll be moving, begin notifying people about your move. Begin by contacting the United States Postal Service and completing a *Change of Address Order* (PS Form 3575). You can do this in person at any U.S.P.S. office, by phone (call 800 ASK-USPS [275-8777]), or online, at https://moversguide.usps.com.

The Change of Address Order has 10 items:

1. Change of Address for: Individual, Entire Family, or Business (choose one)
2. Is This Move Temporary? (yes or no)
3. Start Date (month, day, year)
4. If temporary move, print date to discontinue forwarding (month, day, year)
5. Last Name, First Name
6. Business Name (if applicable)
7. Old Mailing Address
8. New Mailing Address
9. Printed Name and Signature
10. Date Completed

Dream Home Tips

Be sure to inform the Internal Revenue Service of your new address. Call 800 829-3676 or visit the IRS online at www.irs.gov to obtain a Form 8822, *Change of Address*.

In addition to notifying the Postal Service of your new address, you'll also want to inform your friends, relatives, and people and companies you do business with. Consider sending a change of address card (available from the USPS) to the people and organizations on this list:

- Accountant/CPA/financial planner
- Airline frequent flier programs
- Attorney
- Bank(s) and other financial institutions
- Cell phone service provider
- Clubs
- Credit card companies
- Creditors
- Dentist
- Department of Motor Vehicles
- Doctor(s)
- Dry cleaners
- Employer
- Financial companies that manage your investments, retirement account, etc.
- Friends
- Gardener/landscaper
- Girlfriend(s)/boyfriend(s)
- Gym/health club
- Insurance companies
- Internet service provider

Landlord

- Library
- Local and long-distance phone companies
- Newspaper/magazine subscriptions
- Optician
- Parole officer
- Professional acquaintances
- Relatives
- Religious organizations
- School(s)/college(s)
- Social Security Administration
- Union
- Veterinarian
- Voter registration office

Get Ready for Moving Day

Now that your stuff is all packed, your utilities have been turned off, and your mail has been forwarded, you're just about ready to move into your new home! Moving day is going to be hectic as well as exciting, so get a good night's sleep.

Unpacking, setting up your home, decorating, performing minor repairs, and settling in are going to be a long-term process. Until you're settled in, expect to make daily trips to the local hardware store for tools and supplies.

Don't expect to get it all done immediately. Focus on unpacking the most important items and arranging the essential furniture pieces first, such as your bedroom and kitchen.

Hopefully, you'll be comfortable in your new home for a while, so you won't have to think about moving again for many years. You might, however, want to consider refinancing your mortgage at some point if your credit score improves, interest rates drop, or you can obtain better terms on your loan. When you're ready, a mortgage broker can help you with the refinancing process.

Enjoy your new home—and congratulations!

APPENDIX A

Web Site Directory

The following is a list of the web sites and online resources mentioned in this book.

American Moving and Storage Association—www.moving.org

American School Directory— www.asd.com

American Society of Home Inspectors—www.ashi.org

AnnualCreditReport.com—www.annualcreditreport.com

Appraisal Institute—www.appraisalinstitute.org

Bankrate.com—www.bankrate.com

Bankrate.com Moving Calculator—www.bankrate.com/brm/movecalc.asp

Better Business Bureau—www.bbb.org

Budget Truck Rentals—www.budgettruck.com

Century 21 Real Estate—www.century21.com

CityRating.com—www.cityrating.com/costofliving.asp

CNN Cost of Living Calculator—cgi.money.cnn.com/tools/costofliving/costofliving.html

***Consumer Reports* magazine**—www.consumerreports.org

Door To Door Storage and Moving—www.doortodoor.com

Duff & Phelps, LLC, insurance company ratings—www.duffandphelps.com

eBay—www.ebay.com

eMove Moving Referrals—www.emove.com

Equifax—www.equifax.com

Experian—www.experian.com

FHA—www.hud.gov

FICO Score—www.MyFICO.com

FirstGov—www.firstgov.gov

Ginnie Mae—www.ginniemae.gov

Hertz Truck and Van Rental—www.hertztrucks.com

HomeFair.com Standard of Living Calculator—www.homefair.com/homefair/calc/salcalc.html

HomeGain.com—www.homegain.com

Homes.com—www.homes.com

Insurance Information Institute—www.iii.org

Know Your Stuff Home Inventory Program (Insurance Information Institute)—www.knowyourstuff.org

LendingTree.com—www.lendingtree.com

LowerMyBills.com—www.lowermybills.com

MapQuest—www.mapquest.com

Monster Board Salary Wizard—promotions.monster.com/salary

Monster Board Cost of Living Calculator—salary.monster.com/CostOfLivingWizard/layoutscripts/coll_start.asp

Moodys Investors Services insurance company ratings—www.moodys.com

Mortgage101.com—www.mortgage101.com

Mortgage Bankers Association—www.mortgagebankers.org

Move.com—www.move.com

MoveUtilities—www.moveutilities.com

Moving.com—www.moving.com

MyFICO.com FICO Score online—www.myfico.com

National Association of Real Estate Appraisers—www.iami.org/NAREA

National Association of Realtors—www.realtor.com or www.realtor.org

National Flood Insurance Program—www.floodsmart.gov

Newspapers.com—www.newspapers.com

Penske Truck Rental—www.pensketruckrental.com

Prudential Real Estate—www.prudential.com

RE/MAX Real Estate—www.remax.com

Real Estate.com—www.realestate.com

Realtor.com free referral service—www.realtor.com/FindReal

SmartHomeBuy Reports—www.smarthomebuy.com

Space Bag storage packs—www.spacebag.com

Sperling's Best Places—www.bestplaces.net/col/

Standard and Poors insurance company ratings—www2.standardandpoors.com

TransUnion—www.transunion.com

U-Haul Truck Rental—www.uhaul.com

Urgent Business Forms.com—www.urgentbusinessforms.com/purchase_agreement.asp

U.S. Department of Housing and Urban Development (HUD)— www.hud.gov/buying/localbuying.cfm

U.S. Department of Housing and Urban Development (HUD) Real Estate Glossary—www.hud.gov/offices/hsg/sfh/buying/glossary.cfm

U.S. Department of Housing and Urban Development (HUD) HUD-1 Settlement Statement sample—www.hud-clips.org/sub_nonhud/html/pdfforms/1.pdf

U.S. Department of Veterans Affairs—www.homeloans.va.gov

U.S. Internal Revenue Service—www.irs.gov

U.S. Postal Service—https://moversguide.usps.com

USlegalforms.com—www.uslegalfornms.com/contract-for-sale-real-estate.htm

Weather.com—www.weather.com

Weiss Ratings Inc. insurance company ratings—www.weis-sratings.com

Yahoo! Driving Directions—maps.yahoo.com/dd

Yahoo! Real Estate—realestate.yahoo.com/re/neighbor-hood/mail.html

Yahoo! Real Estate Glossary—realestate.yahoo.com/loans/glossary.html

Yahoo! School Reports—realestate.yahoo.com/re/schools/

Zillow—www.zillow.com

APPENDIX B

Glossary

The following is a glossary of important mortgage, credit, and finance terms used throughout this book. Understanding these terms will help you to better find and negotiate your best mortgage or refinancing deal.

Adjustable-rate mortgage (ARM)—A loan with an interest rate that can change during the life of the loan.

If the interest rate goes down, so does the monthly payment (in most cases). If the interest rate goes up, so does the monthly payment. There are several types of ARMs. Some mortgages start off with a fixed interest rate and convert to an adjustable rate after a specified period. The amount the interest rate can change is often subject to a cap.

Amortization—The repayment of a loan, such as a mortgage, in which part of the payment is applied to the principal balance.

AnnualCreditReport.com—A centralized service operated by the three credit reporting agencies (credit bureaus) that processes all requests from consumers who wish to receive their free credit report from each agency.

Annual percentage rate (APR)—The yearly rate of interest that includes all fees and costs paid to acquire the loan (such as interest, mortgage insurance, certain closing costs, and points paid at closing). All lenders are obligated by law to disclose a loan's APR.

Appraisal—An estimate of a property's fair market value calculated by a professional, licensed appraiser.

Broker associate—The person who works for the mortgage broker who is a borrower's primary contact throughout the application, approval, and closing process. Also known as a *mortgage consultant* or a *loan officer*, this person will often work on a commission basis, based on the mortgage products he or she sells.

Cash-out—The process of refinancing and borrowing more money than is owed on a mortgage in order to obtain cash.

Closing—The formal sale of a property and transfer from seller to buyer, when the buyer also formally acquires the mortgage and pays all closing costs and the seller provides the title for the property.

Closing costs—All fees, charges, and taxes the buyer will be required to pay at the closing, including payment for points possibly), taxes, title insurance, and financing costs.

Conforming loan—Any type of mortgage that meets the criteria and limits set forth by the largest buyers of loans, including *Fannie Mae* or *Freddie Mac*.

Correspondent lender—A hybrid company that offers borrowers the benefits of working with a direct lender and the flexibility of working with a broker who represents many mortgage products, typically at more competitive rates than ordinary brokers. A correspondent lender makes approval decisions and initially funds the loan, but then, upon closing the loan, the correspondent lender sells the loan to another lender for servicing.

Credit rating—An educated estimate of a person's creditworthiness, a prediction of the likelihood that the person will pay a debt and the extent to which the lender is protected in the event of default.

Credit report—A credit file disclosure compiled by one of the credit reporting agencies—Equifax, Experian, or TransUnion—

that contains personal and financial information about a person, including name, address, phone number, Social Security number, date of birth, past addresses, current and past employers, a listing of companies that have issued credit to that person (including credit cards, charge cards, car loans, mortgages, student loans, and home equity loans), and details about his or her credit history.

Credit reporting agency (aka credit bureau)—Any of the three national bureaus—Equifax, Experian, and TransUnion—that maintain credit histories on virtually all Americans with any credit history and supply creditors and lenders with timely and reliable financial reports as requested..

Credit score—A mathematical calculation of a person's creditworthiness, in which a credit reporting agency applies a complex formula to his or her current financial situation and credit history. A credit score will be between 300 and 850. The national average is about 678. To qualify for a mortgage typically requires a credit score of at least 620.

Debt consolidation loan—A type of mortgage product that enables a person, by refinancing his or her mortgage, to obtain cash to pay off outstanding higher-interest debt. A debt consolidation loan can be part of a new mortgage or a separate loan using home equity as collateral.

Deed—A written document indicating that a described property is being transferred from the current owner (grantor) to a new owner (grantee).

Deed of trust—A security instrument used in some states, similar to a mortgage, that is recorded in public records, involves three parties—the person borrowing (trustor), the lender (beneficiary), and a neutral third party (trustee) who holds temporary and partial title to the property—summarizes the legal rights of both lender and borrower (including the ability of the lender to foreclose on the property if the loan goes into default), and is canceled when the debt is paid.

Equity—The percentage of the value of a home that the owner actually owns, as distinct from the percentage owed to the lender (through a mortgage, for example).

Fannie Mae—Federal National Mortgage Association (FNMA), a federally chartered enterprise owned by private stockholders that purchases residential mortgages from lenders (thereby providing funds for new loans) and converts them into securities for sale to investors.

Fixed-rate mortgage–A common type of mortgage product for which the interest rate and all monthly payments remain the same throughout the life of the loan, typically 15, 20, or 30 years.

Freddie Mac—Federal Home Loan Mortgage Corporation (FHLMC), a federally chartered corporation that purchases residential mortgages from lenders (thereby providing funds for new loans) and converts them into securities for sale to investors.

Ginnie Mae—Government National Mortgage Association

(GNMA), a government-owned corporation established within the U.S. Department of Housing and Urban Development (HUD) to promote nationwide access to mortgage credit by pooling FHA-insured and VA-guaranteed loans in order to back securities for private investment.

Good-faith estimate—An estimate of all closing fees, including prepaid and escrow items and lender charges, that the lender or mortgage broker must provide to the borrower within three days after he or she applies for a loan.

Home Equity Line of Credit (HELOC)—A type of second mortgage that provides the borrower with a firm commitment from the lender to make a specified amount of funds available for a specified period of time, using the equity in the borrower's home as collateral. During the term of the loan agreement, the borrower can borrow any amount of money up to the credit limit at any time and as often as he or she wants and pay back the outstanding balance over time. The interest rate is adjustable and the interest is calculated daily. A HELOC has an annual fee. This type of loan can be used as a financial safety net that a homeowner taps only when and if it's needed.

Home equity loan—A type of second mortgage that provides the borrower one lump sum of money that he or she must pay back over a specified period of time at a fixed interest rate, using his or her home as collateral. As with a fixed-rate mortgage, the monthly payment on a home equity loan remains constant. Interest rates for home equity loans are typically higher than for mortgages, but lower than for other types of loans, such as credit cards or car loans. The home equity loan has tax benefits, but they're more limited than with a mortgage: Typically, borrowers can deduct interest on home equity loans up to only $100,000. One of the big benefits to this type of loan is that the money can be used for almost anything.

Home inspector—A person experienced, qualified, and often licensed to perform an independent inspection of a home, typically at the buyer's request and expense, to find any major problems before the purchase takes place.

HUD-1 Settlement Statement—A document prepared by the closing agent that details all of the information relating to the sale of the home, including price, amount of financing, loan fees, loan-related charges, real estate taxes due, and amounts to be paid by the seller and the buyer. All of the information on the HUD-1 should correspond to details in the *good faith estimate* and *truth-in-lending statement*. At the closing, both the seller and the buyer sign this document; the lender keeps the original.

Interest rate—In relation to a mortgage, the amount of interest charged on a monthly loan payment, usually expressed as a percentage.

Lender—The party that funds the mortgage and to whom the borrower owes the money—a bank, a credit union, a mortgage company, an investor, or even the U.S. government.

Letter of commitment—A document from the mortgage broker or lender stating that an applicant has been approved for a mortgage, the amount of the loan, and the terms.

Loan officer—The employee of the mortgage broker who is a borrower's primary contact throughout the application, approval, and closing process. Also known as a *mortgage consultant* or a *broker associate,* this person will often work on a commission basis, based on the mortgage products he or she sells.

Loan-to-value (LTV)—The ratio between the value of the property and the amount of the loan. For example, a 20-percent down payment means an LTV of 80 percent and a five-percent down payment means an LTV of 95 percent. Many types of mortgages have a specific LTV as a requirement for approval.

Lock/lock-in—An agreement in which the lender guarantees a specified interest rate on a mortgage for a certain length of time at a certain cost. A rate lock is not a loan approval.

Mortgage—A security instrument used in most states, similar to a deed of trust, that creates a lien on the property that is recorded in public records, involves two parties—the person borrowing (mortgagor) and the lender (mortgagee)—and gives the mortgagor full title to the property and gives the lender the right to sell the secured property if the mortgagor defaults (a sales process called foreclosure).

Mortgage banker—A company that makes home loans using its own money and then sells the mortgages to secondary mortgage lenders such as Fannie Mae or Freddie Mac or investors such as insurance companies.

Mortgage broker—An intermediary between a borrower and a lender. Most mortgage brokers represent multiple lenders and typically offer a broader range of mortgage products than a traditional bank. Mortgage brokers earn a fee for the services they provide. Over 80 percent of home buyers in the U.S. work through a mortgage broker.

Mortgage consultant—The person who works for the mortgage broker who is a borrower's primary contact throughout the application, approval, and closing process. Also known as a *broker associate* or a *loan officer*, this person will often work on a commission basis, based on the mortgage products he or she sells.

Mortgage note—The formal written and legally binding agreement between the home buyer and the lender that states the terms of the loan, includes the buyer's promise to repay the debt, and specifies penalties that could be imposed if payments are late or skipped.

Mortgage preapproval—A commitment from a lender to an applicant for a mortgage, after an in-depth process, assuming that all of the borrower's qualifications remain intact at the time of the purchase and allowing for negation of the preapproval in case of a sudden increase in debt, drop in income, or drop in a credit score.

Mortgage prequalification—An estimate of the size of the mortgage for which an applicant could qualify that a mortgage broker or lender can provides based on the applicant's credit history, credit score, debt, and income. The prequalification process is not binding and does not require the borrower to provide any formal financial documentation or complete a detailed application.

Offer—A formal, written bid to buy that includes the address of the home, the bid, the type of financing to be used, and a target date for closing and occupancy. It should list contingencies that must be met for the offer to be binding. It may be accompanied by a deposit, which may or may not be refundable, depending on the situation. The offer should be made through a real estate agent, although it can be made independently.

Point—A fee the borrower pays to the lender or broker, one percent of the loan amount.

before the end of the term. This is used by the lender as an incentive against refinancing.

Preapproval—See *Mortgage preapproval.*

Prepayment penalty—A fee that a lender can charge the borrower for paying off the loan

Prequalification—See *Mortgage prequalification.*

Prime rate—The interest rate at which commercial financial institutions make short-term loans to borrowers whose credit is so good that there is little risk to the lender. This rate fluctuates based on economic conditions and may differ among financial institutions. The prime rate serves as a basis for the interest rates charged for other loans for which the risk is higher.

Principal—The amount of money borrowed, not including interest, taxes, or insurance premiums associated with the mortgage.

Private mortgage insurance (MPI)—Policy typically required by lenders of borrowers applying for a conventional mortgage but unable to pay 20 percent down, which guarantees the lender will be paid even if the borrower defaults on the loan. The lower the down payment, the higher the cost of this insurance, which is added to the monthly payment. Once the borrower owns at least 20-percent equity in the home, this insurance can be canceled and the mortgage can be adjusted accordingly.

Purchase and sale agreement—A written and legally binding contract that both the buyer and the seller sign, outlining the terms, conditions, contingencies, and timetable for the sale of a property and describing the rights of the buyer and the seller pertaining to the transaction.

Real estate agent—A person who is licensed in a specific state to negotiate and arrange for the sale of real estate.

Realtor®—A licensed real estate agent who is a member of the National Association of Realtors®.

Refinance (aka refi)—The process by which a mortgagor pays off a loan with the proceeds from a new loan, typically using the same property as security for the new loan. The goal is typically to obtain a lower interest rate, reduce the monthly payment, shorten the duration of the loan, or cash out some of the equity.

Rescission period—Three full days after receiving all required disclosures and signing loan documents in which a borrower is allowed to cancel a refinance mortgage. Federal law allows this cancellation (rescission) period for certain loan transactions secured by the borrower's home, but not for loans made to purchase, construct, or acquire a primary residence or to transactions secured by a secondary residence or rental property

Second mortgage—A loan a homeowner can obtain in addition to his or her primary mortgage. Just as with a primary mortgage, the home is used as collateral. This second mortgage is totally separate from the first mortgage, with its own rate and terms. The lender for the second mortgage is not entitled to any proceeds from the sale of the home until the lender on the first mortgage has been repaid. Because the risk of default is greater, rates for second mortgages tend to be higher than for first mortgages.

Sub-prime borrower—A person who doesn't meet the approval guidelines for a prime rate mortgage, due to a below-average credit score, a negative credit history, lack of employment information, the inability to provide various financial documents or verifiable income, or even a bankruptcy.

Sub-prime lender —A lender or mortgage broker specializing in working with sub-prime borrowers and that offering a range of home financing options with less strict or nontraditional approval guidelines.

Truth-in-lending statement (TIL)—A document provided by a lender to a mortgage applicant that details information about the mortgage, including the estimated monthly payment and all of the costs associated with the loan, including finance charges. If any of these figures change prior to the closing, the lender will revise the TIL and provide the update to the buyer at the closing.

Index

A

Actual cash value coverage, 156
Address change notices, 193–195
Adjustable-rate mortgages
  basic features, 72–74
  interest-only options, 87
  potential disadvantages, 33
Affordability of mortgages, 30, 48, 173
Agency agreements, 107
Agency disclosure documents, 98
Agents (insurance), brokers versus, 157
American Moving and Storage Association web site, 184
American School Directory web site, 123
American Society of Home Inspectors web site, 136, 138
Amortization
  of interest-only loans, 84–85, 87–88
  principles of, 70–71
AnnualCreditReport.com web site, 8
Annual percentage rates, 34
Application fees, 165
Application process, 24, 62–65
Appraisal Institute web site, 136
Appraised values, 129
Appraisers
  fees, 164–165
  functions of, 18–19, 134, 135
  in home purchase process, 24
  web sites, 136
Approval guidelines, variations among, 46
Asking prices, 129, 133–134
Assumable loans, 89–90
Attorneys, 20, 163
Auto movers, 189

B

Balloon mortgages, 75–76
Bankrate.com web site, 21, 39
Banks, approval standards of, 47
Best practices of lenders, 38
Better Business Bureau, 38
Bidding wars, 143–144
Binding quotes for moving, 182
Biweekly mortgages, 76–78
Box buy-back services, 190

Breaking leases, 177–178
Brokers (insurance), agents versus, 157
Brokers (mortgage). *See* Mortgage brokers
Budget Truck Rentals web site, 187
Buyers' agents, 97, 108

C

Cable TV charges, 192
Cash deposits, 146
Century21.com web site, 113–114
Certified checks, 164
Change-of-address notices, 193–195
CityRating.com web site, 21
Climate, as decision factor in home buying, 119
Closing costs, 166
Closings
  mistakes to avoid, 170–173
  overview, 160–163
  preparing for, 163–164
CNN.com web site, 21
Commissions, 96–97, 107
Community newspapers, 126
Commuting, as decision factor in home buying, 119
Comps, reviewing, 133–134
Consumer Reports web site, 157
Container movers, 185–186
Contingencies, 129, 130, 131
Contracts, importance of understanding, 152
Convertible ARMs, 73
Correspondent lenders, 55–56
Corsetto, Joseph, 137–143
Counteroffers, 132
Credit card applications, 12
Credit problems, 61, 78–83
Credit reporting agencies, 3, 7
Credit reports
  changes in, 12–13
  discrepancies between, 11–12
  improving, 36
  lenders' use of, 9–10
  obtaining copies for review, 7–8
Credit scores
  benefits of knowing, 8
  changes in, 12–13, 14
  defined, 3–4
  discrepancies between, 12
  lenders' use of, 9, 12
  minimum requirements, 66–67
  standards for, 9–10
Crime rate, as decision factor in home buying, 124

D

Debt ratio, 7, 45
Debts, evaluating, 3, 6, 44
Debt-to-income ratio, 45
Decisions, rushed, 109
Deeds of trust, 168
Department of Housing and Urban Development (HUD), 38, 92
Deposits with offers, 146
Dirty Little Secrets from the Credit Bureaus, 13
Discount points, 90
Documentation
  agency disclosures, 98
  of all agreements, 173
  home inspection, 140–141
  loans available without, 81–82
  purchase and sale agreements, 148–152

required for applications, 63–65
required for closing, 163–164
reviewing at closing, 167–170
reviewing prior to closing, 163
Do-it-yourself moves, 186–189
Door To Door Storage and Moving, 185
Down payments
ability to afford, 3
comparing for mortgages, 35
loans available without, 82–83, 88–89
loan-to-value ratios and, 91
low-percentage, 15, 84
prequalification questions, 43–44
typical requirements, 15
Dry settlement, 161
Duff & Phelps web site, 157
Duration of loans, impact on payments, 70

E

eBay, 179
eMove.com web site, 189
Employment
avoiding changes before closing on loans, 170
need to show, 14
prequalification questions, 44
Equifax web site, 3
Equity
as homeownership benefit, 16, 18
interest-only loans and, 84, 86–87
Escrow accounts, 171
Escrow closings, 160
Ethics for Realtors, 104–105
Expenses, calculating monthly totals, 3, 5
Experian, 3, 10
Extensions to lock-in agreements, 60
Extra payments, 77, 78

F

Fair Isaac Corporation, 11
Federal Housing Administration (FHA) loan program, 15, 83–85
Fees
cable TV cancellation, 192
at closings, listed, 164–166
comparing for mortgages, 34
home inspection, 140
including in purchase negotiations, 145
lender discretion on, 60–62
lock-in, 36, 60
mortgage insurance premium, 84
negotiating, 35–36, 145, 167
for obtaining credit scores, 8, 10
of real estate agents, 96–97, 107, 109
statements of, 52–53
truck rental, 187
FHA loans, 15, 83–85
FICO scores, 11, 12. *See also* Credit scores
Final walk-throughs, 162–163, 171
Financial calculators, 2, 71
Financial information, providing to brokers, 56–57
Financial situation, assessing, 2–7
Fixed/adjustable mortgages, 72–73
Fixed-rate mortgages, 69–72, 87
Float down policies, 36, 60
Flood insurance, 154
Form 4506, 169
Formal offers, 129–132

Full-service movers, 180–184
Future plans, as decision factor in home buying, 119

G

Geographic areas, selecting, 23
Ginnie Mae web site, 2, 17
Giordani, Mark
  on application process, 62–65
  on ARMs, 74
  on assumable loans, 90
  on bad brokers, 65–66, 67–68
  on balloon loans, 76
  on biweekly mortgages, 78
  on credit scores, 66–67
  on FHA loans, 84–85
  on fixed-rate mortgages, 71–72
  on interest-only loans, 86–88
  on interest rates and broker fees, 59–62
  on loans without income verification, 79–82
  on mortgage broker selection, 53–59
  on no-down-payment loans, 82–83
  on VA loans, 89
Good faith estimate statements, 52, 53
Guaranteed or extended replacement cost coverage, 156

H

Hard-money loans, 81–82
Hertz web site, 187
Home buying
  appraisals and inspections, 134–143
  assessing personal needs, 125
  checklists for, 100–101
  choosing location, 119–125
  learning home's value, 128–129
  negotiating prices, 129–134, 143–146
  purchase and sale agreements, 148–152
  web sites, 113–119
  without agents, 112
  working with real estate agents, 96–100, 103–112
Homegain.com web site, 39
Home inspectors
  acting on reports of, 141–142
  functions of, 19, 134–136, 172
  importance of hiring, 109–110, 138–139
  licensing, 139–140
  selecting, 136–137, 140–141, 142–143
Homeowners' associations, 119–120
Homeownership
  assessing readiness for, 2–7
  benefits of, 16–18
  planning questions, 21–22
  professional help for achieving, 18–20
  steps in achieving, 22–25
Homeowner's insurance, 153–154, 155, 156
Homes.com web site, 114–115
Home tour checklists, 100–101
Home warranties, 154–155
Honesty in application process, 64–65
Honesty of mortgage brokers, 32
Hourly rate quotes for moving, 182
HUD-1 statements
  elements of, 53, 164, 166

online copy, 164
reviewing with other disclosures, 52
HUD workshops, 38
Hybrid ARMs, 73

I

Income
calculating, 2, 4
need to show, 14
obtaining loans without documenting, 79–82
prequalification questions, 43
Inquiries, impact on credit scores, 14
Inspections prior to closing, 162–163, 171. *See also* Home inspectors
Insurance agents
functions of, 19, 24–25
selecting, 152–153
Insurance coverage, 152–158, 171
Insurance Information Institute web site, 153, 157
Interest-only mortgages, 85–88
Interest rates, 35, 60–62
Internal Revenue Service, change-of-address notification, 193
Internet. *See* Web sites

J

Job changes, avoiding before closing, 170

L

Landlords, notifying of move, 177–178
Leases, 177–178
Lender inquiries, impact on credit scores, 14
Lenders
commitment letters from, 161
correspondent, 55–56
finding, 30–37
insurance requirements of, 155
selecting, 37–40
sub-prime, 69
LendingTree.com web site, 39
Letters of commitment, 161
Liability insurance, 154
Licensing of home inspectors, 139–140
Living standards, as decision factor in home buying, 124
Loan officers, 32
Loan origination fees, 62, 165
Loan-to-value ratios, 61, 91
Locations, selecting, 119–125
Lock-in agreements, 36, 59–60
LowerMyBills.com web site, 39

M

Major purchases, avoiding before closing, 170
Market prices, 20–21, 123
MIP fees, 84
Mistakes in closing documents, 170
Monster Board web site, 21
Monthly expenses, 3, 5
Monthly income, 43
Monthly payments
for ARMs, 72
with interest-only loans, 85–86, 87–88
relation to loan term, 70
Moody's Investors Services web site, 157
Mortgage101.com web site, 91

Mortgage Bankers Association, 38
Mortgage brokers
  finding, 30–37
  functions of, 19, 31, 33, 54
  selecting, 37–40, 53–59
  unethical practices, 37, 65–66, 67–68, 168
Mortgage comparison shopping sites, 39
Mortgage insurance premiums, 84
Mortgage notes, 167
Mortgage par rates, 40
Mortgages
  ability to afford, 30, 48, 173
  describing in P&S, 151
  prime versus sub-prime, 68–69
Mortgage types
  adjustable-rate, 72–74
  assumable loans, 89–90
  balloon, 75–76
  basic considerations in selecting, 50–52
  biweekly, 76–78
  for borrowers with imperfect credit, 78–83
  fixed-rate, 69–72
  interest-only, 85–88
  prime versus sub-prime, 68–69
  VA loans, 88–89
  varying approval standards among, 46
Move.com web site, 115–116
MoveUtilities, 192
Moving.com web site, 116
Moving out
  do-it-yourself moves, 186–189
  hiring movers, 180–186
  packing supplies, 189–191
  packing tips, 178–179
  preparing for, 176
Multiple Listing Service (MLS), 103

N

Name affidavits, 168
National Association of Real Estate Appraisers web site, 136
National Association of Realtors, 99, 103–104, 113
National Flood Insurance Program web site, 154
Negotiations
  closing fees, 167
  lease settlements, 177–178
  over formal purchase offers, 131–132, 143–146
  prequalification advantages for, 29
  Realtor fees, 107, 109
Neighbors, as decision factor in home buying, 120
Newspapers, 126
Newspapers.com web site, 126
No-documentation mortgages, 81–82
No-down-payment loans, 82–83, 88–89
No-income-verification loans, 80
Nonbinding quotes for moving, 182
Not-to-exceed quotes for moving, 183

O

Occupancy affidavits, 168
Offers, procedures for, 129–132
Online financial calculators, 2, 71
Option loans, 88
Overage, 35

Owner's title policies, 135

P

Packing supplies, 189–191
Packing tips, 178–179
Paperwork. *See* Documentation
Parking, as decision factor in home buying, 120
Par rates, 40
Payment letters, 168
Pay option loans, 88
Pay stubs, 63
Penske Truck Rental web site, 187
Personal finances
  assessing, 2–7
  discussing with Realtors, 111
  providing information to brokers, 56–57
Personal needs, in home purchase decision, 125
Piano movers, 189
Pick-a-payment loans, 88
Pickup-and-delivery movers, 184–186
PITI, 6
PITIO, 6–7
Points, 34, 90–91, 165
Postal Service change-of-address forms, 193–195
Preapproval, prequalification versus, 40–42
Prepayment, benefits of, 77
Prepayment penalties, 174
Prequalification
  advisability of, 57
  preapproval versus, 40–42
  process overview, 42–47
  rationale for, 28–30
Prequalification analysis, 45–46
Prices of homes, evaluating, 128–129
Prime loans, 68–69
Principal, 53
Private mortgage insurance (PMI), 83, 169
Property taxes, 123–124, 165–166
Prudential.com web site, 116–117
Purchase and sale agreements
  elements of, 148–152
  in home purchase process, 24
  trying to withdraw from, 68, 149

Q

Quotes for moving costs, 182–183

R

Ratings of insurance companies, 156–157
Real estate agents
  functions of, 19–20, 23, 96–97
  help in learning home's value, 128
  Realtors versus, 94, 104–105
  representation, 172
  role in negotiations, 145
  selecting, 102–103, 105–106
  working with, 96–100, 103–112
Real estate attorneys, 20, 163
RealEstate.com web site, 117–118
Real estate taxes, 123–124, 165–166
Real estate web sites, 113–119
Realtor.com web site, 98
Realtors
  functions of, 19–20
  qualifications, 99, 103–104
  real estate agents versus, 94, 104–105
  working with, 103–112

Recasting, 87
Referrals
  to full-service movers, 181
  to mortgage brokers, 55
  to real estate agents, 97–98
  from Realtors to other professionals, 108
Refinancing, 174, 196
Rejected offers, 131
RE/MAX web site, 117
Renter's insurance, 185
Renting, homeownership versus, 16–18
Replacement cost coverage, 156
Request for Copy of Tax Form, 169
Rights to terminate clauses, 151
Round table closings, 160

S

Safety, as decision factor in home buying, 124
Salary Wizard, 21
Sale subject to a mortgage clauses, 151
Savings
  assessing, 3, 5
  for down payments, 15
  prequalification questions, 43–44
Scams, mortgage broker, 37, 67–68, 168
Schools, as decision factor in home buying, 120–121
Self-service movers, 184–186
Sellers' agents, 97, 103, 107–108, 172
Seller's disclosure statements, 151
Similar home prices, 133
SmartHomeBuy.com web site, 134
Space Bag storage packs, 179
Sperling's Best Places web site, 21
Standard and Poor's web site, 157
Standard of living, as decision factor in home buying, 124
Stated income/stated asset mortgages, 79–80
Stevens, Thomas, 96–100, 103–112
Sub-prime borrowers, 69
Sub-prime lenders, 69

T

Tax-deductible interest, 16
Taxes paid at closing, 165–166
Tax returns, 63
Terminology, 92
Time frames
  for application process, 62–63
  for closings, 162
  for house hunting, 25, 95, 110
  to lock in rates, 59–60
Title insurance, 135, 153
Total income, calculating, 2, 4
Total interest, relation to loan term, 70
Trader Publishing Company, 114
Trans Union web site, 3
Truck rental, 187–189
Truth-in-Lending statements, 52

U

U-Haul box packages, 190
U-Haul web site, 187
Unethical practices, 37, 65–66, 67–68, 168
Urgent Business Forms.com web site, 148
USlegalforms.com web site, 148
U.S. Postal Service change-of-address forms, 193–195

Utility companies, contacting, 191–192

V

Variable-rate mortgages. *See* Adjustable-rate mortgages
Verbal agreements, 173
Veterans Administration (VA) loan program, 88–89

W

W-2 forms, 63
Waiver of rights clauses, 152
Walk-throughs, final, 162–163, 171
Warranties, 154–155
Web sites
  AnnualCreditReport.com, 8
  Better Business Bureau, 38
  checking for market prices, 21
  FHA, 84
  FICO scores, 11
  Ginnie Mae, 2, 17
  home buying, 113–119, 129
  home inspectors, 136, 138
  HUD, 92
  insurance company ratings, 157
  Insurance Information Institute, 153
  legal forms, 148
  Mortgage101.com, 91
  Mortgage Bankers Association, 38
  mortgage comparison information, 39
  National Association of Realtors, 98, 105, 113
  National Flood Insurance Program, 154
  Newspapers.com, 126
  resources for moving, 180, 184, 185, 189
  SmartHomeBuy.com, 134
  truck rental, 187
  Veterans Administration (VA), 89
  Weather.com, 119
Weiss Ratings Inc. web site, 157
Wet settlement, 161
Withdrawing offers, 132
Worksheets, personal finance, 4–6

Y

Yahoo! Real Estate web site, 21, 92, 118
Yahoo! School Reports web site, 123
Yield spread premiums, 40

Z

Zillow.com web site, 118–119, 129

Other Entrepreneur Pocket Guides include

How to Sell Collectibles on eBay

How to Sell Toys and Hobbies on eBay

Start Your Real Estate Career

Start Your Restaurant Career

Mortgages and Refinancing: Get the Best Rates